VICTORY WITHOUT SWORDS

The Story of

Pat and Lily Okura

Japanese American Citizens
in 1941 America

Robert B. Kugel, MD

EAGLE EDITIONS
2009

EAGLE EDITIONS
AN IMPRINT OF HERITAGE BOOKS, INC.

Books, CDs, and more—Worldwide

For our listing of thousands of titles see our website
at
www.HeritageBooks.com

Published 2009 by
HERITAGE BOOKS, INC.
Publishing Division
100 Railroad Ave. #104
Westminster, Maryland 21157

Other books by the author:
Exodus Unwanted

International Standard Book Numbers
Paperbound: 978-0-7884-3144-9
Clothbound: 978-0-7884-8069-0

VICTORY WITHOUT SWORDS

Dedication

This book is respectfully dedicated to Kiyoshi Patrick Okura and Lily Arikawa Okura and the 110,000 persons of Japanese ancestry who were evacuated from their homes and interned in assembly centers and relocation camps during World War II.

VICTORY WITHOUT SWORDS

TABLE OF CONTENTS

VICTORY WITHOUT SWORDS

List of Illustrations

VICTORY WITHOUT SWORDS

PREFACE

Americans of one type or another have always been associated with wars. Many persons suffer hardships during wars, though some never come to light and some are glossed over as the events which produced them fade into history. Stanley Baldwin, a former prime minister of the United Kingdom, once remarked that wars would end if those who were killed in wars were to come back to life again.

Although many stories depict hardships suffered and endured by American citizens, one not often told is the internment of Japanese American citizens who were living on the West Coast during World War II. These were ordinary people, literally routed out of their homes and sent first to Assembly Centers and later to Relocation Camps, where many spent the four years of the American involvement during World War II. They had committed no crimes, but the discriminatory feelings in the country against them, especially on the West Coast were so powerful that President Franklin Roosevelt in 1942 was induced to issue an executive order that all persons of Japanese ancestry should be interned. These internment camps turned out to be like the concentration camps of Europe. This biography of Pat and Lily Okura is about one such family.

Robert and Dorothy Kugel

VICTORY WITHOUT SWORDS

Introduction

Mankind seems to have been given to wandering. Earliest traces of man in Africa and the Middle East bear out this trend. It is not always clear why various migrations took place. Sometimes migrating to another place was probably in order to find better sources of food, shelter and water. At other times escape from pestilence was the cause for migration as man tried to evade the harsh realities of living. Simple curiosity about the world served to motivate some migrations. The ravages and upheavals of war caused other migrations to take place such as those which occurred during and after World War II.

We know little about when and why some of the waves of people from other lands and cultures took place and why some came to America. Invariably the newcomers were resented by those who were already there.

Who We Are - Where We Came From

"Our families were just ordinary people. We were just like a lot of other immigrant families who came to America hoping to find a better way to live," both Pat and Lily Okura would say.

Americans are apt to point out that we are a nation of immigrants. From our earliest history many of those who immigrated were decidedly unhappy with the situations from whence they had come. Their hope was that a new life in a new world would be an improvement. Some immigrated because of despotic political regimes. Others left due to religious persecution. Still others were virtually forced out of their homelands because of severe famine.

Once they arrived in the United States, they were often subjected to new and different hardships and were seldom well received. The early English settlers in Virginia and in Massachusetts endured great privation during their first years. The Spanish immigrants in Florida fared no better. The Native American people were curious but less than enthusiastic about the arrival of European immigrants.

Later generations of immigrants faced the same difficulties. The waves of Europeans, Germans, Polish, Italians, Irish and others, who arrived in New York and other Atlantic seaboard cities during the second half of the 19th Century found not only no welcoming arms, but no housing and no employment. Usually it was find your own way or die in the attempt, and many did die soon after arrival.

Most of the stories about American immigrants center on the East Coast, but the situation on the West Coast was the same. Immigrants from Asia and the Pacific Islands had been induced to come to America in the latter part of the 19th Century where they helped to build the railroads, to work the mines and to plow the fields. Frequently they found living and working in America to be brutal. Later when some of them brought their families, they found that locating housing of any sort was usually difficult, if not impossible and obtaining social services of any kind was impossible.

When the economy became gloomy with the end of the gold boom and the declining fortunes of the railroads in the West, Asian people were blamed for the difficulties, none more than the Japanese.

All ethnic groups have legends and lore about their origins, and the Japanese people have a rich and at times fanciful heritage about their origins. Although some of the early legends about the origin of the Japanese islands and the Japanese people are questionable so far as authenticity is concerned, they figure significantly in the nature and lore of the people. It is said that twin gods, Izanagi and Izanami, were commanded by the gods to establish the islands, and they did so by shaking over 4,223 drops from a jeweled spear, which is the number of islands constituting present day Japan. Only 600 are inhabited today. The twins married each other and produced offspring who became the Japanese people, an occurrence reported to have been about 600 BC although there is very little solid evidence for this date. At about this same time the present imperial dynasty of Japan was also established and it is alleged to be the only dynasty which has ever existed.[1]

While contemporary science suggests that the Japanese islands were formed by a series of earthquakes, volcanoes, and floods, the early legends figure prominently in the belief system of many Japanese people. Major influences for the society which emerged came from the much older civilization of China. Later many crafts were introduced from

Korea in the Third Century AD. By the end of the12th Century the capital at Kyoto had a population of 500,000.

. Of great cultural and historical importance was the arrival of Buddhism from China in the early sixth Century AD, approximately 500 years after its introduction in China. Buddhist beliefs and doctrines of piety, peacefulness, and obedience helped to mold the Japanese character from this period of time to the 17th Century. Later Shinto beliefs were superimposed and became another important religious system which emphasized respect and worship of ancestors, especially the emperor. Portuguese style Christianity was introduced by St. Francis Xavier in 1549 AD and spread rapidly, a matter of some concern for the Imperial Court. Later various Protestant groups in Japan established many small enclaves of their brand of Christianity.

A system of war lords or military dictators called shoguns emerged, reducing the power of the emperor and establishing a feudal society. At different times in the history of Japan the emperor and his court were very weak. The authority of the shoguns was effected by the establishment of well-disciplined warrior knights known as samurai. A feudal caste system developed, which consisted of the samurai as the dominant group but also included artisans of all types, peasants and merchants.

The shoguns were successful in warding off invasions from Korea and Kublai Khan from China in the 13th Century. In addition they sharply limited the influence of the Christians.

In an effort to reduce outside influences the shoguns and the emperor resisted all efforts by Europeans and other Asiatics to influence their country. These efforts virtually sealed Japan from the rest of the world. Not until 1853 when Commodore Perry, heading a fleet of US Navy warships, forced the Japanese government to allow an opening of the country to American trade did western ways become dominant. Extensive political and social changes resulted with the establishment of the Meiji government in 1868.

Some historians believe that the seeds for war between the Japanese and the Americans which came a century later were sown at this time.

Despite efforts to minimize outside influences, extensive modernization, including industrialization resulted. Heightened concern developed in the 19th Century about how to thwart the emerging influence of Russia. These concerns were largely ones coming from the newly empowered ruling classes. War with Russia broke out in 1905, and after the devastating battle of the Sea of Japan, Japan emerged as the dominant force in the East. Shortly afterwards in 1910 Japan annexed the kingdom of Korea. Japan was now a significant force in the East.[2]

Western education, science and technology were introduced, and many Japanese accepted these new ways and ideas with alacrity. Even those who attempted to retain their earlier customs were affected by western thoughts and ideas. These vast changes in the mores of the people and the industrialization of the country substantially altered the nature and structure of the society in Japan. No longer was it certain that one would always have a job or remain in the same prefecture as one's family had done for generations.

Major urban areas such as Tokyo emerged. As a result of these changes, a certain amount of dissatisfaction arose among all groups of people but especially the younger population.

Just as in Europe, many young men looked to America as a place where opportunity was thought to be unlimited. America seemed to them to be a place where periodic wars were less frequent. Unlike the Chinese immigrants, Japanese men often immigrated with families. The story of the Okura and Arikawa families is fairly typical of the Japanese immigrant families. This is a story about how these two fairly typical families fared in America. When the first generation of Japanese Americans known as Issei had arrived, they met and overcame many adversities. Animosities towards persons of Asiatic background had grown steadily from the last third of the 19th century through the first third of the 20th century.[3] Greater intensity occurred prior to the entry of America into World War II.[4]

The smoldering animosity and discrimination towards Japanese Americans was fully unleashed towards them following the bombing of Pearl Harbor in 1941 and the subsequent entry of America into World War II.

Life started out for Pat Okura and Lily Arikawa in much the same way as it did for many Americans. They were born into hard-working, middle class families, Pat in Los Angeles and Lily in Santa Barbara, California. In much the same manner that all children learn, they came to understand in a variety of ways who they were and where they had come from. Friends and relatives and the shopkeepers of local businesses were persons mostly of Japanese ancestry. The first generation of Japanese Americans were known as Issei and the second generation, Nisei. At about six years of age they entered regular public schools and here they interacted with and learned about other children who came from different backgrounds.

Frequently during childhood, older family members would relate stories about where they had come from. Pat's father, Momota Okura, (born in 1882 and died in 1964), came from Nakamaki in the prefecture of Okayama. Momota, along with a few other young men, all veterans of the Russo-Japanese war of 1901-1905, wanted to leave Japan to get away from war and all of its hideous aspects. By chance they met up with an older gentleman, a banker and a financier, Mr. Hiromasu Katayama, from Okayama, Japan.

In 1905 Mr. Katayama sold all his possessions with the intent of emigrating to the United States with his two children and a tutor. He offered passage to America to Momota Okura and two other young bachelors.

Most Japanese in those days came to the West Coast, especially to California. Mr. Katayama, however, arranged that they would go to Texas to grow rice. Not being a citizen, he was unable to buy land, but he leased 500 acres of land east of Houston in Matagordo County, near Bay City, Texas. He then bought 200 mules to work the land. Momota remained in Texas for five years and, by working hard, became reasonably prosperous.

Eventually he saved enough money so that he began to think he was in a position to get married. In the early 1900's most of the young Japanese men and women had arranged marriages. Mr. Okura went back to Okayama City in Japan, where the details of the marriage were worked out. He was introduced to Fuyuko Emi (born in 1888 and died in 1953), who was also from Okayama. They were married in 1910 and returned to Texas a year later.

On coming to Texas, Fuyuko Okura was extremely unhappy. She berated her husband for telling her that Texas was beautiful and a wonderful place to live. She thought it was desolate compared to Japan and wanted to return to her homeland.

After a year of unhappiness and complaining, eventually Momota acceded to her request. Taking what money and possessions they had, they returned to Los Angeles to await the next ship to Japan. As ships sailed to Japan only about every three or four months, they had to wait until passage was available.

However, when Fuyuko Okura soon found out that she was pregnant, the trip was canceled and they decided to remain in Los Angeles. Their first child, Pat, was born September 26, 1911. Seven other children, four boys and three girls, were also born in the United States. (It was not until 1937 that Fuyuko got her wish to return to Japan for a visit.) They settled down to become a typical hard-working, goal-oriented family in Wilmington, California, the harbor area of the rapidly developing city of Los Angeles.

Pat said, "My parents were married in 1910. My father was 26 years old when they married. Altogether there were eight of us. We spoke both Japanese and English at home.

"My father was active in the Japanese community. He was president of the local Japanese Association in San Pedro and also served on the board of directors of the Central Japanese Association in Los Angeles. Since he and all Japanese immigrants who were born in Japan could not become citizens of the United States, they were all designated as aliens, ineligible for citizenship as a matter of federal law.

"They organized Japanese Associations in communities where substantial numbers of first generation Japanese (Issei) resided. My father and Lily's father were both presidents of the Japanese associations in their respective communities of San Pedro and Long Beach and were friends.

"My father was also president of the Okayama Kenjinkai, a Russo-Japanese War Veterans Association composed of men who resided in southern California. The Kenjinkais were made up of residents from various prefectures in Japan. This association served as the welfare and human service agencies for Japanese citizens who were from their various prefectures.

"My father was part of a group of businessmen who organized The Okayama Kenjinkai, which was a type of welfare system for the Japanese American community. When people needed help with food, jobs or housing, they could always count on getting assistance, including financial help if that was what they required. Nobody in their Japanese-American community was ever on public welfare.

"Later the Congressional Committee on un-American Activities, headed by Representative Martin Dies, accused my father before and during World War II of raising money for the Japanese government."

"My family had settled in Santa Barbara," Lily said. "I was the second child, born January 20, 1919. My father, Mr. Sadao Arikawa, purchased a grocery store but sold it and later started working in an insurance business where he soon became financially successful. We moved to Long Beach when I was three years old and my sister, Yayoi Ono, was five." Lily's father (born in 1885, died in 1976) and her mother, Masaye Mori (born in 1892, died in 1981) met each other in California. Sadao Arikawa was from Kagoshima-ken and Masaye Mori was from Wakayama-ken in Japan. This was a second marriage for Masaye Mori, her first husband having died following a ruptured appendix.

In certain aspects Lily's family differed from Pat's family. For one thing, her parents became acquainted when they were young living in California. Lily said, "Just like other young people in the area my parents dated and went together to various community activities and to movies. There were no arranged marriages in the Arikawa family. When my parents became United States citizens in 1953, they changed their first names to Tom and Mary, to accommodate to the mores of the average Americans. The Arikawas were Christian, and there was a fair amount church-related activity in our family."

The Arikawa family fortunes flourished so that Lily and her sister, Yayoi Ono (born in 1917, died in 1985), lived a very comfortable middle class life in the city of Long Beach. "I had many advantages as a child which many of my friends were unable to enjoy. We had many parties, dances, piano and violin lessons," Lily said.

In 1929, when Lily was 10, the family took an eight-month trip to Japan. Lily said, "While in Japan, I was exposed to Japanese dancing and learned to play the koto, a 13 stringed instrument, and the samisen. In 1998 I donated my koto to the TOHO KOTO Society of Washington, D.C."

Noting her delight in music, her father on returning to California, bought her a piano so she could take lessons. It was not long until she became reasonably proficient as a pianist. Lily and her sister took piano lessons for $5 an hour. Lily also studied ballet.

"We were a close family," Lily added. "On the weekends we would usually have family outings. Frequently on the weekends, we went to the beach and put up a tent, where we would spend the day. I was not very athletic, but my father, who loved baseball, organized a baseball team and we went to most of the games, which were held on the weekends. When I was older, I did some bit parts in the movies, one of which was Marco Polo. For a time I was a stand in for Anna May Wong. In 1936 I represented the city of Long Beach in the Rose Bowl parade."

As a young child Lily went to Japanese school on Saturdays to learn the language and customs of Japan.

"We spoke Japanese at home about half of the time," she said.

Most of Mr. Arikawa's customers were farmers. These farms were mostly small and were located along the Pacific coast. He not only sold them insurance, but he would often help them with other matters, such as buying certain books that they might want or helping them with documents and papers which people needed to have translated. He had a thriving business and was helping members of the Japanese American community.

Athletics were an important pastime among these teenagers. When he was 15, Pat first met Lily, who was seven at the time. Lily's father had organized and directed a baseball team, called The Long Beach Nippons. He put this baseball team together, bought all of the equipment and then he managed the team. Pat was a good player and ended up on the team.

Every Sunday they played baseball. Sometimes they went to Santa Barbara, Guadeloupe, San Jose, or other places to play baseball. Whole families, including their children, would show up at the games. Many girls attending were considered attractive to those young players. Pat once said, "I wondered why Mr. Arikawa always brought along his two daughters, who were about 9 and 7 years old at the time." They served as the score keepers for the team.

"I had a good time in high school," Pat said. "I was a good student as well as a good athlete, and I was mostly well accepted. I felt little discrimination as an Asian American in Wilmington, California, where I attended grade school and high school. Only two Japanese American families were attending schools in Wilmington. In schools where the number of Japanese-American families was greater there was considerable anti-Japanese American feeling. I was elected the most outstanding athlete and outstanding student when I graduated from high school. One particular episode of discrimination occurred around graduation. Two of us, a Mexican American girl and myself were both honor

students. We were told that only one minority student could
sit in the front row at graduation exercises. I sat in the second
row."

After high school, Lily went to Long Beach Business
College (now Long Beach State College), where she graduated
with a bachelor's degree in business administration in 1939.
She also attended Lakewood Junior College. "I thought   I
needed some marketable skills so I   took accounting
and typing. At one time I managed a tea room in Long
Beach," Lily said.

.   Many years later during 1953-55, when Lily and Pat were
living in Omaha (1942-1970), Lily resumed her interests
in business by taking advanced courses in administration at
the University of Nebraska at Omaha. Her older sister was
always helping other people.

After graduating from high school, Pat went to the
University of California at Los Angeles (UCLA), where he
graduated with a bachelor's degree in 1933 and a master's
degree in Psychology in 1935. Persons of 'Asian ancestry,
African-Americans and criminals' were not allowed to buy
property or to live in Westwood, the section of the city to
which UCLA had recently moved, and where it is still
located. There was a property covenant against them.
Both the Asian-Americans and African-Americans
profoundly resented being classified along with criminals,
the implication being that they were all one and the same.

Persons born in Japan could purchase property and
homes, but usually the title to the property was in the
name of an adult child who was an American citizen by
reason of birth.

These restrictive covenants were not lifted until 1968.
Elsewhere in Los Angeles Japanese Americans could not
become citizens at that time.   They were labeled aliens and

were, therefore, ineligible for citizenship, unlike aliens from other parts of the world.[5]

To get an education, Japanese-Americans had to put aside these concerns. For Pat this situation meant having to hitchhike eight miles to and from UCLA every day. Among other accomplishments Pat was the first Japanese American to earn a letter in baseball while attending UCLA.

At first Pat wanted to go into medicine, but discrimination against Asian Americans was high. It was generally understood that each of the medical schools on the West Coast would admit only one Asian American each year. Pat was accepted at some out-of-state medical schools but the combined expense of tuition and living away from home was too great. He then decided instead to take advanced work in psychology.

Pat was also the first person of Japanese ancestry to be accepted to do graduate work in psychology at the University of California at Los Angeles, where he obtained a master's degree in psychology in 1935. His first job was as a civil service employee doing some research for the Los Angeles County Department of Welfare. He did psychological research in tests and measurements to design proper civil service tests for use in the county.

Two of his professors, Dr. Grace Fernald and Dr. Ellen B. Sullivan, were helpful in obtaining positions for him after graduation. Dr. Fernald had been doing remedial work with children who were thought to be mentally retarded. Most of this effort was directed to learning how to help these children with reading, writing, and spelling. The kinesthetic method of teaching reading was used for some of these children. Through the efforts of these two professors at UCLA, he was able to make various contacts which would be helpful later on in his life.

Many young Japanese American men who graduated from studies in engineering or architecture at Stanford or the University of California at Los Angeles, for example, were unable to find jobs in their fields anywhere in southern California. Many of these young men would take the only jobs they could find and ended up in low paying jobs as unskilled workers in shops and stores. Given this situation, Pat decided on a career in psychology. Pat took a Civil Service position as a research assistant for the County of Los Angeles. It paid well, about $ 300 a month, and it was what he wanted to do.

Before the bombing of Pearl Harbor, Pat worked as a personnel technician in the Los Angeles City Civil Service Department. Pat's Japanese name was Kiyoshi, but the clerks at the Department had difficulty in spelling and pronouncing his name. One of them decided that Okura was really an Irish name, O'Kura, and therefore he should have an Irish first name as well, like Patrick. His official records then listed him as Patrick.

Later Pat decided to take a job with the Japanese American Citizens League (JACL) chapter in Los Angeles. As executive director, he was in charge of recruiting new members, which would enable new chapters to be formed in the East Los Angeles, West Los Angeles and the surrounding Japanese American communities. This activity took place towards the end of the Depression years when interest in JACL had fallen off because business had become so impoverished throughout the area that funds were often not available for people to join such organizations.

As a result of growing anti-oriental feeling, California in 1913 adopted laws prohibiting "aliens ineligible to become American citizens" from becoming citizens. The Japanese American Citizens League, therefore, insisted on primary emphasis on the term citizens, because those persons who were born in this country were citizens.

Pat got the idea of having a big festival in 1936 and 1937 with the intent of bringing Japanese American families together again. This event he hoped would in turn renew or establish their interest in the Japanese American Citizens League.[6]

Events included many kinds of activities such as Japanese dancing and various cultural programs like flower arranging and origami construction. Nisei week was organized in an effort to demonstrate and promote various crafts. In addition there was a talent show which included singing and dancing. In 1937 and 1938 an attractive young lady from Long Beach showed up for the talent show. This lady was Lily Arikawa, 18 years old. Pat told people he was her uncle because he thought that he, all of 26, should not be seen with such a young girl as his girl friend.

Lily was a beauty queen of Long Beach at the time. Their renewed friendship led to courtship and eventually to their marriage on October 19, 1941 in a Buddhist Temple. The service was a mixed Buddhist and Christian one. When Pat was a teenager, he was baptized in a Presbyterian church by the pastor, Rev. Louis Evans, Sr.

The young couple had a honeymoon in New Orleans. On returning to Los Angeles, they had only a brief time as newlyweds living in a new home and were dreaming of the future. All of this contentment changed abruptly with the Declaration of War against Japan, Germany and Italy in December 1941. By April 1942 they found themselves interned in an Assembly Center located in the old SantaAnita Race Track, where they spent the next eight months. An era of relative tranquillity was at an end.

How Life Began To Change

Both Pat's father and Lily's father had been active in the Japanese community. They had been presidents of the Japanese associations in their respective communities. These associations were known for helping people with various personal matters and especially   promoting acceptance of civil rights for Japanese American people and achieving for them full citizen rights as guaranteed by the United States Constitution.

In 1919 shortly after World War I was concluded, Japanese Americans found that there would be little change in their lives despite the high flown statements surrounding the Treaty of Versailles. President Wilson called for self-determination of all groups. It soon became clear that he was addressing only the problems of European peoples and certainly not Asiatic or African people in the United States. At the Versailles peace conference Japan called for a statement endorsing a principle of racial equality. This request was denied.

Many first-generation Japanese immigrants or Issei who were well educated in their professions and had obtained licensure in the states where they lived found that they had great trouble becoming established as they were regarded as aliens. Although they confined their practices mainly to Japanese communities, they wondered about what would happen to their children who were born in the United States and therefore were citizens by right of birth.

They asked themselves these questions many times. In San Francisco there were problems of schooling. Parents of second-generation students were told they would need to send their children to the Oriental School in Chinatown. After a court fight, this order was changed, and some of the Nisei children were allowed to attend regular neighborhood schools.

In an effort to bring like-minded Japanese American people together Dr. Thomas T. Yatabe, Mr. George Togasaki and Ms. Kay Tsukamoto of San Francisco began meeting to explore what could be done to establish rights to which they felt they and their children were entitled. After much discussion concerning the name to be used, an organization called the American Loyalty League of San Francisco was organized in 1921.[1] Other chapters were organized around the San Francisco bay area and also in Seattle, Fresno and other California cities. At best these early organizations were only marginally successful in obtaining recognition of their rights as US citizens. Several leaders thought a national convention to establish aims and objectives would be in order. The National Council of Japanese American Citizens Leagues was organized and they held a first meeting in Seattle, but little came of these efforts.

Ten years later another effort was made to consolidate these several groups. A strong chapter had developed in Los Angeles and eventually a major convention was held there in 1930.

Although many young Nisei were being educated in science, education, medicine and law in US colleges and universities, they often found it difficult and usually impossible to secure good positions in their various communities. Quite naturally they asked questions to the effect of 'what good is my American citizenship if I am denied entrance in the work community; what protection does it offer?'

These and other issues were among the features which led to the formation of the Japanese American Citizens League. Several chapters in California and one each in Oregon and Washington came together to form the organization.   Finally in 1930 in Seattle an all embracing organization, the Japanese American Citizens League (JACL), came into being. At this first convention there was a pledge of allegiance, presentation of the colors and a singing of America.[2]

One of the early issues of discrimination considered by JACL was the Cable Act of 1922, sponsored by Representative John Cable of Ohio. It provided that an American woman would lose her citizenship by marriage to an alien. It was not until 1931 that some of this offensive language was altered.

Another case was that of Tokutaro Slocum who was born in Japan but raised in North Dakota. Although aliens were exempted from military service in World War I, he volunteered. While serving in France, he filed for naturalization. His petition was turned down. At one point the Supreme Court ruled that naturalization was restricted to "free white persons, to aliens of African nativity and to persons of African descent." Various veterans groups helped his cause with petitions and meetings with Congressional officials. Finally in 1935 the Nye-Lea bill signed by President Roosevelt reversed this bit of discrimination by allowing World War I veterans of Oriental birth to obtain full citizenship.

At first people of the older generation did not join JACL, though later on many of them changed their minds about the organization and did join. They were always doing something for the community. This same concern about the rights and needs of people was part of every day life in their respective households and greatly influenced Pat and Lily in what they would do later in their lives. From the onset as an organization JACL did not discriminate against women. Young girls were encourage to join JACL and to participate in their programs. There were times when the Issei and Nisei did not agree on methods for obtaining their rights as citizens. Many of the Nisei were anxious to become much more vigorous in their demands for recognition of their capabilities whereas many of the older generation were willing to accept matters as they were.

Both generations always proclaimed their loyalty to the United States. A young student, George Kyotow, in San Francisco wrote, "Our ideas, customs, mode of thinking, our whole psychology is simply American. Physically we may be Japanese, but culturally we are Americans."[3] Japanese teachers in the schools were urged to learn more about American ways, and demands were made that textbooks should stress the American environment. The members of the second generation or Nisei wanted to retain the virtues and culture of the Japanese race which they thought were important aspects to becoming better and more valuable American citizens.

In 1943 while being held as an internee by the US Government, Pat's father, Momota Okura, was considered for deportation to Japan, though nothing so severe actually happened to him. Nevertheless, some people were actually deported. Whole families would decide to go back to Japan if the father of the family was to be deported because they did not want the family to be separated. Those who were forced to go back lost their American citizenship. The people who were sent back to Japan had nothing. With the war going on, Japan did not want them, nor did the United States.

During this period of time JACL was attempting to be more effective in obtaining legislation which was beneficial to the Japanese-American community. Mr. Saburo Kido who was serving as JACL president from 1940 - 1946 was aware that alone he could not accomplish all of the objectives which

JACL now set before themselves. He persuaded the Directors to hire a full time executive assistant. Eventually Mr. Masaru "Mike" Masaoka from Utah was hired.

Losing no time in getting to work, Masaoka testified in Los Angeles about why Nisei were being refused jobs in the defense industries. As a result of this effort many Nisei were hired but once war was declared all of these advances came quickly to an end. By January 1942 Congressman Clarence Lea of California demanded that "all Japanese, whether citizens or not, be placed in inland concentration camps."[4]

After the war, the JACL was instrumental in persuading the Congress of the United States to restore their citizenship. As a result some of the families came back to the United States. Some of the younger Japanese Americans thought their elders had sold out to the government by cooperating. They thought they should have been more militant with protest marches and sit ins.

The history of discrimination in the United States against persons of Asian ethnicity was intense and pervasive. As early as 1848, for example, many Chinese immigrants had come to the United States during the California gold rush days. They worked, sometimes as indentured servants, in mines, fisheries, railroads and many other industries. By 1859 after the gold rush was over and the economy had taken a turn for the worse, children of Chinese ancestry were excluded from the public schools in San Francisco.

Other laws and practices made life difficult for many persons of Asian background.[5] Although about 90 % of the labor used to complete the first transcontinental railroad in the United States, the Union Pacific, was performed by Chinese and Japanese laborers, little recognition has been given to their contributions.[6] When an economic collapse occurred in California in 1876, they became scapegoats.

Congress passed the Chinese Exclusion Act in 1882[7] which prohibited further entry into the United States of Chinese laborers. Due to strong feelings against children of Asian parents, the San Francisco School Board in 1906 passed resolutions whereby children of Chinese, Korean and Japanese ancestry were to be sent to Oriental public schools and could not attend the regular schools.[8]

In 1913 the California Alien Land Act prevented Asians from purchasing land. After both houses of the US Congress passed the legislation known as the Oriental Exclusion Act, it was signed in May 1924, by President Coolidge. These were two of the most extreme and restrictive laws concerning Asian heritage.

Only in 1943, with the passage of the Magnuson Act, was the Chinese Exclusion Act repealed. In 1952 the Walter-McCarran Act conferred the rights of naturalization and eventual citizenship for Asians not born in the United States.[9]

When the Executive Order Number 9066 (Fig. 1) was signed by President Roosevelt requiring all persons of Japanese ancestry to be interred, JACL met and agreed to the peaceful acceptance of the terms included in the order.[10]

Lily said, "My mother went first to a Relocation Camp at Jerome, Arkansas. She was later transferred to Crystal City, Texas, in order to be with my father. My father had been transferred to Crystal City, which was a prisoner of war camp. It is interesting to recall that the camp at Crystal City was where the government of Peru sent a group of Japanese Peruvians. Peru was not at war with Japan so it was hard for us to understand why were they were sent to America.

"It seemed that the United States government wanted to have some people to exchange. These people did not come because they wanted to. Later they were declared ineligible for reparation. They were excluded from receiving the $20,000 settlement from the United States government which had been made available by the passage of the Civil Liberties Act of 1988. It was distressing to observe all the behind the scenes activities of the federal government during World War II."

The End of Tranquillity - Pearl Harbor and the Aftermath

Like most American families on that fatal Sunday of December 7, 1941, Pat and Lily were shocked, horrified and confused by the news of the bombing of Pearl Harbor. What it was to mean to them and to the Japanese-American community was beyond their wildest imagination. The next, even bigger bombshell for the Japanese-American families, was their second "day of Infamy," which came on February 19, 1942 when President Roosevelt signed Executive Order No. 9066[1] giving the US Army jurisdiction over the lives of persons considered to be Japanese aliens and their children all of whom were American citizens by birth. This term was interpreted to include any Asian-American and all of those of Japanese ancestry.

Over 117,000 Japanese-Americans who were living in California, Oregon and Washington State on the west coast and part of Arizona were affected. Japanese-Americans and Japanese aliens elsewhere in the country, including Hawaii, were not included. At no time were any charges leveled at any of the Japanese-Americans, either citizens or aliens, living on the West Coast. No trials were ever held, but incarceration awaited about 120,000 men, women, and children.

The Army selected Lieutenant General John L. DeWitt to be in charge of the assembly centers which on the west coast were located mostly in race tracks and county fair grounds. It was General DeWitt who had said, "Once a Jap, always a Jap." These assembly centers were used while awaiting construction of permanent facilities which were called relocation camps. Altogether there were 14 assembly centers and later there would be 10 camps. The camps were scattered in the remote desert and mountain areas in Arizona,

Colorado, Arkansas, Wyoming, Utah and two camps in Eastern California.[2]

Pat related, "On that Sunday morning of December 7, I played golf with my father-in-law, Mr. Arikawa. On the way home, it was announced on the radio that war had been declared. At about three in the afternoon agents from the Federal Bureau of Investigation entered the house and took Lily's father away with them. That night, shortly after midnight, they took my father away from his home. Approximately 2,000 men were removed from their homes and families over December 7 and 8. All these people had been active as community leaders. We remember being very upset, indignant, confused and angry."

Later that night many who had been prominent in Japanese-American activities were picked up for interrogation by agents from the Federal Bureau of Investigation. About 2,000 Japanese men in all were apprehended on the night of Pearl Harbor. They were said to be the most 'dangerous' of the Japanese aliens and were considered to be agents of the Japanese government. For this group of men, as with all others, no formal charges were ever made and trials were never held.

After the bombing of Pearl Harbor the long, smoldering animosity towards Asians in the United States burst into flames. While the feelings against all Asians were high, the greater anger by far was directed towards persons of Japanese ancestry regardless of whether they were born in America and therefore were citizens by virtue of birth. White supremacists found it easy to shift their animosity from African-Americans to Japanese-Americans. For example, Senator Thomas Steward of Tennessee stated that the Japanese were, "cowardly and immoral....different from Americans in every conceivable way and should have no right to claim US citizenship." He went on to say, "taking an oath to this country would not help. They [the Japanese] do not believe in God and have no respect for an oath." Then Congressman John Rankin from Mississippi stated, "This is a race war....The white man's civilization has come into conflict with Japanese barbarism....It is of vital importance that we get rid of every Japanese, whether in Hawaii or on the mainland."[3]

In 1944 the federal agents who were detaining both Mr. Okura and Mr. Arikawa held hearings concerning their activities. Mr. Okura was being considered for deportation to Japan. After three days of testimony Mr. Okura was found to be innocent of the various charges that he was an espionage agent for the Japanese government. He was sent to the Missoula Relocation Center in Montana, where his wife and youngest child had been interned since October 1942. Mr. Arikawa was sent to a Prisoner of War Camp at Crystal City, Texas. Later his wife, who had been sent to the Jerome Relocation Center was permitted to join him at Crystal City.

Lily added, "My father used to like to go fishing and went to San Pedro on the breakwater at Terminal Island to fish almost every Sunday after playing golf. Periodically he had noticed that strange people were asking him and others about what he was doing, but we did not understand why these people were asking all these questions. They apparently thought that men, like my father, who were leaders in the Japanese American community, would become leaders of a group that might become informers."

On December 7 Lily had been spending the afternoon at the beauty shop on Terminal Island, near Wilmington, where many Japanese- Americans did a lot of fishing. Pat called her, asking her if she could get home. She said, "Of course, I can get home. I have my own car." At this point she had not heard about the bombing of Pearl Harbor, which had taken place earlier in the day.

She was astounded and shocked when Pat told her that Pearl Harbor had been bombed and that war with Japan was declared. Lily then tried to leave to go home but was stopped on Terminal Island, just off Long Beach, by the armed Immigration authorities, telling her that she could not leave the island. Much later, about two am, she was finally released and permitted to go home, after being photographed ("mugged") and finger printed.

The round-up of these Japanese-Americans took place on the day and immediately following the bombing of Pearl Harbor. Thus it seemed clear to them that the FBI had already identified, located and marked many of these Japanese American men. Mr. Arikawa was taken first to the Los Angeles County jail.

When Lily tried to contact her father in jail, she was barred from seeing him. The woman where she inquired said to her, "You're as guilty as the old one. You ought to be in jail as well."

Lily, who was very close to her father, could only cry when she was finally permitted to see him. She noticed that his glasses were bent and he had some scratches on his head which had been inflicted when they brought him to the jail. In looking back, Lily remembered that all her father said to her then was, "Pat called me 'Dad' today when he left me." Pat had become the son Mr. Arikawa had never had. Later they would learn how he and others were insulted and beaten.

Pat's father was apprehended that same Sunday night. He was taken to Pat's house about 11:30 PM after being interrogated and searched in his own home. He was accompanied by FBI agents and police officers from the Los Angeles Police Department who came to the house. They searched the entire house looking for documents and other material which they thought would indicate that he was an espionage agent.

When Pat asked what right they had to come to his house, he was informed that they had been deputized by the Federal Bureau of Investigation to make searches. These officers then searched through the house and gathered up books, papers and whatever they could find in the house written in Japanese to use as evidence which they thought would serve as an indication that they were dealing with subversive persons.

Pat's father had several books from Japan about the Russo-Japanese War. All such books published in Japan at the time always had a picture of the Emperor of Japan in the front. The newly deputized FBI agents concluded that having the Emperor's picture in a book meant that they were Japanese sympathizers and therefore were subversive. They took Pat's father away at this time, and Pat and Lily did not see him again for over two years. Along with others he was sent to a camp in Missoula, Montana. After they learned where he had been sent, they were able to write and receive letters. However, the letters were always censored.

Strange conclusions were drawn about what was considered evidence of subversive activity. In 1937 when a Japanese general came to Los Angeles, Pat had been asked to show him around the city. This visit was used as evidence of Pat's intent to be subversive. It was later suggested that Pat's father was trying to organize veterans of the Russo-Japanese war to be agents for Japan.

Immediately after Pearl Harbor and the declaration of war, many Japanese American young men from the area who were initially interred, volunteered to join the Army and were accepted. Mostly, these young men were placed in positions which were non-controversial. Many went on to serve with great distinction, and some were killed in battle, including one of Pat's brothers. Pat's family thought it was ironic to have a son killed when they were being accused of being disloyal.

War against Japan had been declared in December 1941. However, Congress under the leadership of Representative John Tolan held hearings in February 1942 in Los Angeles regarding the safety of the local citizens and determining what the next course of action should be. Although later it became clear that the decision to remove persons of Japanese ancestry had already been made, the hearings were held anyway so citizens could express their opinions. At the last pre-internment convention of JACL in San Francisco a decision was made that JACL would cooperate in this whole evacuation procedure. It was the feeling of the JACL leaders at the time that no one could do anything about changing the evacuation orders, so people should go peacefully and avoid riots.[4]

The leaders would try to work out the best deal possible. Today, some of the Issei and Nisei (Japanese living in America but born in Japan and second generation of native born Japanese-Americans) are being criticized by the Sansei, Yonsei. and Gosei (third, fourth, and fifth generations of Japanese Americans), who, of course, were not born at that time. They say, "Why did you give up without a fight?" Others say, "The JACL encouraged the government to put us away."

Lily pointed out, "We had no support in those days. We were a small group, and we did not have the support of the public. California was anti-Japanese to begin with. Some of the younger people do not seem able to comprehend such an action."

With the war on, Japanese-Americans were constantly

being harassed. For example, Pat who had been in charge of giving certain qualifying examinations to job applicants for the Los Angeles City Civil Service Department, was accused of being unfair in the administration of these examinations. Some of the applicants turned down for these positions when they failed the examination said they could not understand his instructions. Though he spoke fluent English, and, in fact, he knew no other language, he was nonetheless accused of being unfair.

On February 18, 1942, the then mayor of Los Angeles, Fletcher Bowron, called Pat to his office to request that he resign. Pat was incensed and refused. He pointed out that he had a civil service position and as such his legal rights would require that formal charges be made and that he should be given a hearing. The hearing never took place. A newspaper reporter said that he had infiltrated the Civil Service Department with Japanese-Americans and that his plan was for them to take over the department.[5]

Pat indeed had encouraged some young people to take the civil service examinations and some did. In all about 50 Japanese-Americans, out of 20,000 employees, were working in the various city departments at that time. All of them had taken and passed the qualifying examinations, none of which Pat had administered. Thirty-seven of them were women who were in various clerical appointments and were hardly in a position to do anything of a subversive nature. Pat was ultimately given a leave of absence from his civil service position. However, after the war when he inquired about the possibility of returning to this job, he was told that the position had been eliminated as a line item from the budget and, therefore, was no longer available. At one time there was an inflammatory front page article in the Los Angeles Times, quoting Drew Pearson, which declared that Pat Okura was intent on subverting the department by bringing in young Japanese Americans whose intent was to take over the running of the Department. He was also declared to be one of the most dangerous persons in the United States at the time.[6]

Meanwhile, plans were being drawn up by the US Army to remove all Japanese Americans from the West Coast. In March 1942 posters (Fig. 2) were placed over the area stipulating that all persons of Japanese ancestry were to be interned. The definition of being Japanese was one- sixteenth Japanese blood. Everyone would first be required to go to a designated assembly center.

The Okuras were given four days to be at the assembly center. People were told that they could take one duffel bag of belongings and nothing more. No mattresses were to be brought along. At the center they were given a bag of straw to make their own mattresses at the center. The assembly center to which Pat and Lily were assigned was the old Santa Anita Race Track, located in Arcadia. Other places used were Bay Meadows Race Track and the Fair Grounds. An extensive description of the assembly centers and the relocation centers in various parts of the western United States has been released by the National Park Service of the Department of the Interior.

Altogether there were 15 assembly centers located at Puyallup, Washington, Portland, Oregon, Marysville, Sacramento, Tanforan Racetrack near San Francisco, Stockton, Salinas, Merced, Pinedale, Fresno, Tulare, Santa Anita Racetrack, Los Angeles, Pomona, in California, and Mayer, Arizona.[7]

These assembly centers were phased out to be replaced by 10 relocation centers located at Manzanar in Owens Valley in eastern California, Poston in Arizona, Tule Lake in northeastern California, Minidoka in south central Idaho,

Heart Mountain east of Cody, Wyoming, Granada in southeastern Colorado, Topaz in central Utah, Gila River southeast of Phoenix, Arizona, Rohwer and Jerome in bottom lands in Arkansas.[8]

All but the Arkansas center were located in semi-desert country. The relocation centers were primitive, having been hastily constructed. Most of the barracks consisted of tar paper shacks with no insulation, hot in the summer and freezing in the winter. Some of the quarters were only tents at the time of the arrival of the first group of evacuees. Many of the evacuees came from southern California with only light weight clothing for summer or winter. When they reached places like Heart Mountain in Cody, Montana, they were not only quartered in inadequate facilities but they had little or no winter clothing suitable for the harsh conditions found in winter.

In many ways Japanese-Americans before the war had been accepted as part of the community. They were recognized as being hard-working, conscientious people. In schools their children did well academically. It was heart-breaking to them to be referred to in the newspapers as the "Yellow Peril."

The section of Los Angeles, then known at Little Tokyo, was essentially closed.[9] Businesses were sold or fell into ruin with no one to operate them any longer.[10] By the end of May 1942 all of the people of Japanese ancestry had been cleared out and all businesses were closed. Many of these businesses were taken over by African-American persons.[11]

Many families were forced to sell homes, possessions and other property at great losses. After the war, some people regained their property, but many did not. To these people the internment camps were as degrading and humiliating as the infamous Nazi concentration camps in Europe.

These centers were run as prisoner of war facilities. Barbed wire enclosures surrounded the facilities; guard towers were on every corner; searchlights played about the camps constantly; and the facilities were constantly patrolled by soldiers who had orders to shoot anyone attempting to escape.[12] One elderly man was killed because he came too close to the enclosure. Two-thirds of those evacuated were citizens of the United States and not one of them had been charged with a disloyal act. Many young men volunteered to join the Army or Navy. By the close of the war this number was about 40,000. Many served with distinction.

Life in the Santa Anita Assembly

As the Western Defense Command of the US Army had
been given jurisdiction over the assembly centers, everything
was done 'Army style', complete with mess hall, barracks,
and latrines. The Hilton it was not. At Santa Anita horses
were out and Japanese-American internees were in.

Before the assembly centers were operational, a curfew
was imposed on all Japanese-Americans. Everyone had to
be at home by 8 PM. If people had jobs that would keep
them out after this time, they had to have special permission
to return home after hours. In addition, everyone had to
remain within five miles of their home, and exceptions were
infrequently made. The first evacuees in Los Angeles came
from the harbor area and gradually more came as the
authorities rounded up people by geographical areas
of residence, reaching out in ever enlarging concentric circles
from the harbor.

The last of the evacuees came to Santa Anita in May
1942, bringing the total number to 19,000. Hoping not to be
mistaken for Japanese and trying to avoid being sent to the
centers, some Chinese and Korean people wore buttons on
their clothes which read, "I'm Chinese" or "I'm Korean."

Everyone of Japanese ancestry in his area of the city
received notification that they would have 30 days to move
to the Santa Anita Race Track, located in Arcadia, just
outside Los Angeles. As newlyweds of five months, it came
as a major blow to Pat and Lily when they were told they
would have a stable measuring about eight feet by ten feet for
their home. The fresh asphalt poured on top of the manure
and urine soaked dirt floors could not overcome the powerful
stench of the stables. "Coming to the assembly center at
Santa Anita after being married only five months left us

disgusted, discouraged, apprehensive and confused," Pat and Lily both said.

Lavatory facilities were minimal and hopelessly inadequate to say the least. The latrines were the open trench variety with no privacy partitions. For the men this arrangement was not too bad but for the women it was extremely embarrassing, degrading, undignified and humiliating, producing major indignation among them. Initially there were only nine showers for first 7000 people. Folding Army cots with mattresses filled with straw were not much better than sleeping on the floor.

They were told they could bring one duffel bag of possessions with them; everything else had to remain, including their homes, their stores and shops, furniture and, of course, their livelihood. Pat and Lily, like others, made arrangements to have someone look after their property. Some were able to rent their homes, but many were not and property issues became a major concern of the internees. Some Japanese-American citizens were able to have their property returned to them after the war, but many were not so fortunate.

At the Santa Anita Assembly Center conditions soon became chaotic. Bickering among the groups was almost constant. The internees were constantly wondering why they had been singled out for such indignities. They had not committed any crimes so why were they being treated as though they were criminals? Parents were at a loss to know how to answer these and many other questions which were raised by their children.

To the internees it seemed that all one did during the day was first line up for breakfast which no sooner ended until one lined up for lunch and then dinner. About 3,000 people were assigned to each of six or seven mess halls.

The food was not bad, but it was heavy in dairy products, potatoes, bread and meat, especially ham. This diet was not the type of food to which Japanese-Americans, especially the older generation, were accustomed. They wanted rice, fruit, and vegetables. Among the internees were at least 100 people who were cooks, dishwashers and butchers. Some of the leaders went to the Army authorities to request that they accept the responsibility for the food preparation. This request was accepted, and for many of the people life began to look more hopeful after they assumed these functions.

These workers were paid $ 8, $ 12, or $ 16 per month depending on their skills. Physicians caring for people received only $ 16 per month. People were given $ 3 a month for clothing. This pay discrepancy was hard to accept when the internees worked side by side with Caucasian workers who had the same educational background but who were paid standard wages for the times.

Lily and Pat had been assigned to what was a tack room or groom's area. Although a small room, it offered them somewhat more privacy than others had. To make their own quarters more attractive, Lily used some tea towels which she had brought with her to make curtains to provide a modicum of home like appearance. In remembering these days, Lily said, "I always like to have things nice. That's just the way I am. So the curtains were a must for me." In keeping with this point of view, Lily was one of the few women who always wore a dress and high-heeled shoes despite comments from some of the other women who thought she was 'putting on airs.'

Other people put up cloth partitions between the toilet stalls to offer more privacy. However, the stables were still stables, open at the top so that at night if a baby cried or if a

family were arguing, everyone in that section was disturbed
and upset. Maintaining individuality was almost impossible
since everybody knew what was taking place in their
neighbor's unit.

The plan from the start was to use the assembly centers
as temporary quarters until more permanent camps could be
completed. All the relocation camps were located in remote,
fairly desolate places. One such place was Camp Jerome in
Arkansas, situated in a swampy area. All were complete
with watch towers, searchlights and high fences in the same
manner as a prison or concentration camp, and armed guards
patrolled constantly. Most of the Okura and Arikawa family
members were sent here.

The camps were surrounded by barbed wire fences, and
guards on the walls pointed their guns towards the inside of
the camp. They were told that the guards were for their
protection. To these confused and discouraged people it was
hard to understand why the guns were pointed towards them
rather than towards the outside. How were those on the
inside being protected?

Some of these camps had a visitor house where friends
could come. The house was divided with a screen partition
with the internee on one side and the visitor on the other,
another example of the prison-like atmosphere.

The Japanese-Americans referred to them as
their concentration camps, American style. About 70 % of
the internees were native-born American citizens of Japanese
ancestry.

Among the many factors which seemed especially unfair
to the Japanese-Americans on the West Coast was that no
other ethnic groups in the country were singled out for similar
treatment. German-Americans and Italian-Americans were
not harassed, and they certainly were not driven into camps

even though the United States had declared war on both Germany and Italy. Japanese-Americans elsewhere in the country were never subjected to these same indignities.

When Pat entered the Assembly Center, he was determined to do nothing to facilitate any of the activities. He was bitter, resentful, angry and disgusted and vowed that he would do nothing to help the war effort. However, he had brought books with him, some of which had to do with the principles of self-government.

While studying these books and at the same time observing the continuing bickering among his people, he thought it should be possible for this group of people to govern themselves in some measure if they were given the opportunity. He suggested that each section of the camp should elect a leader, and in turn they would establish an organization with a chairman to negotiate with the Army authorities. Pat and a small group of JACL leaders divided the camp into 13 districts and held elections to form a Board of 13 Councilmen. When this plan was accepted, Pat was elected to be the representative from their area and later elected as the chairman of the whole group.

With her background in business, Lily was asked to become the secretary for Mr. E. J. England, the director of education and recreation for the center. One day a request came to Mr. England from the Archdiocese of Los Angeles as a result of an inquiry by Father Flanagan, the organizer and director of Boys Town outside Omaha, Nebraska. He wrote to see whether some Japanese-Americans might be available to fill recently vacated jobs at Boys Town.

Altogether he had eight positions for people who could work as poultry men, carpenters, gardeners, and various jobs of this sort. Pat and Lily were quickly able to identify these people who would meet the specifications. Mr. England was anxious to obtain outside jobs for both Lily and Pat. Other requests came in from elsewhere in the country so that some people had the opportunity to leave the center.

With the nation at war the demand for food was growing. Some of men at relocation camps close to agricultural areas were given the opportunity to work on the farms. Since many of these men were familiar with farming, they became a great asset to local farmers. How ironic it must have seemed that these young men had been forced off their land when they were rounded up for inclusion under the orders of General DeWitt.

Meanwhile most of those who had come to the assembly center at Santa Anita had been moved to various permanent camps around the country, where most of them would remain until the end of the war. The trip to Arkansas, for example, took about five days. Each train load consisted of about 500 people. On the journey they were in cars where all the blinds were pulled day and night so they could not observe the scenery. Many people from the Santa Anita Assembly Center had been transferred to various relocation centers which had been established around the country.

Late in the summer of 1942, Father Flanagan of Boys Town, Nebraska, indicated that he wanted a psychologist who could do some testing of some children at Boys Town. Pat was encouraged by Mr. England to send his credentials to Father Flanagan, which he did, but he heard nothing for a few months.

Finally Pat was offered the position of psychologist, which he accepted and was told a suitable position would be available for Lily as well. However, the arrangements for getting to Omaha were not completed until the early fall. Pat and Lily were the last to leave the Santa Anita Center as they had signed up to be "key" personnel. They would be the last to go. They went to Boys Town, Nebraska.

The areas where the camps were located were in places where anti-Japanese sentiment was high. When people arrived at the relocation camps, they were assigned to barracks. Many people lost belongings precious to them, such as family pictures and books. Their assets were frozen.

After the war some of the internees could not talk about what had happened to them. For many of them the great strength in their lives was their churches and temples. The American Friends Society protested the whole governmental action which had taken place and was the first outside group to offer help to these Japanese-Americans.

Some of the camps had 'special' groups of internees. For example, about 350 'resisters' were sent to Heart Mountain at Cody, Wyoming. These were people who did not accept the internment process promulgated by the federal government. People classified as trouble makers were sent to Tule Lake. As a facility it was not closed until 1946. By this time most of the other camps had been closed.

After Executive Order 9066 was issued, Eleanor Roosevelt expressed her objections. She visited several of the relocation camps and once remarked, "To undo a mistake is harder than not to create one initially."[1]

Shortly after everyone left, Santa Anita reverted to being a race track. Pat and Lily were originally lined up to be sent to Jerome, Arkansas, but on their very last day at Santa Anita, travel arrangements to Omaha came through. All their belongings were sent to Jerome, Arkansas. On October 31, 1942, Halloween, they arrived in Omaha, free to move on to a new life.

In her book, _The Invisible Thread_, Yoshiko Uchida[2] writes tenderly about a similar series of events from the point of view of a young Japanese-American girl. This book offers further understanding about the difficulties and indignities .which were endured by Japanese-American people. Another description of conditions at the camps is contained in the story provided by James Hannon in his novel *Nasakenai (We Are Forsaken)* In this novel the author describes the indignities, confusion and resignation of these people.[3]

Reflections on Boys Town, Nebraska

Before leaving California, Pat and Lily had been given one day to spend in Long Beach prior to taking the train for Omaha. Many thoughts rushed through their minds as they pondered on what to expect. Would they ever return to their early home, they wondered. They wandered about looking for some old familiar places. Neither Lily nor Pat had been out of California, except for the trip Lily had taken to Japan when she was young and their honeymoon in New Orleans. Going to the Midwest was a big adventure which began with the three-day train trip from Los Angeles to Omaha.

By the time they arrived in Omaha, five families from Santa Anita had already come to Boys Town so they were not alone. At first they were housed in a section of the convent. This arrangement seemed quite inappropriate to them so another place was found on the main Boys Town campus, but this, too, proved to be unsatisfactory. Subsequently they were provided housing across the street from Boys Town in what had been a motel.

Although they knew little about Father Flanagan or Boys Town before coming to Omaha, Father Flanagan proved to be an inspiration to both Pat and Lily. His philosophy of offering a second chance to these boys, who through no fault of their own, found themselves without family and without any help but in great need, was inspirational. Pat could use his background and skills in psychological testing at once, for which he was pleased. He also could engage in counseling as part of the efforts to rehabilitate these young boys, most of whom were classified as delinquent.

He soon came to appreciate Father Flanagan's famous slogan, "There's no such thing as a bad boy." Pat's relationship with Boys Town lasted for 17 years.

Lily was asked to be a secretary, a position which she accepted, but she soon wanted to change in order to utilize more of her skills. An opportunity arose which allowed her to become involved with the Young Women's Christian Association (YWCA). In this capacity she learned more about the community of Omaha and the people of Nebraska.

She eventually became the administrator of the C. Louis Meyer Therapy Center, a rehabilitation center for children with various types of disabilities, located on the University of Nebraska College of Medicine campus and affiliated with the University of Nebraska. In this capacity Lily learned still more about the community and also about ways to help many of these children with multiple disabilities.

These were the war years, and feelings against Japanese-Americans, whether citizens or not, ran high in Omaha as elsewhere in the country. In some sectors of Omaha Father Flanagan was soon scorned because of his protection of Japanese-Americans. He was labeled a "Jap lover" because he had taken in several Japanese-Americans from the assembly centers.

Father Flanagan never demurred and was constant in his praise of his Japanese-American workers for their first-rate work and their contributions to the efforts of Boys Town. At one point a newspaper article taunted Father Flanagan by suggesting that he should fly the Japanese flag at Boys Town.

Later through the efforts of Father Flanagan, Pat's parents were able to come to Boys Town. For a time Pat's father did work in the laundry. After the war, the elder Okuras rented a house close to where Lily and Pat resided, and they settled in Omaha. Aided by Father Flanagan, Pat and Lily managed to get about 300 families relocated to Omaha.

During some of his early years at Boys Town, Pat was

often asked to talk to various civic groups about his experiences and those of other Japanese-Americans. Not surprisingly, in 1947, he helped organize a chapter of the JACL. Father Flanagan became a charter member of the local JACL.

Throughout the war years and afterwards many continuing difficulties confronted the Japanese-American communities so far as obtaining the rights and privileges provided to other Americans and guaranteed under the US Constitution.

One such issue was related to a small but vocal group of Japanese-American men who felt strongly about being interned and who refused to sign an oath of allegiance before joining the Army. The first two questions on the application they were asked to sign, were "Would you serve in the Army and would you swear loyalty to the United States?" They would answer 'no' to both of those questions and so they were called the 'no, no' boys.

These men were subsequently tried in court and sent to the Army prison at Ft. Levenworth, Kansas. Eventually they were released and through the efforts of JACL and their convictions were overturned and erased from their records.

Curiously, many other Japanese-Americans who had accepted the orders for internment were ostracized for having anything to do with the "no, no" boys. They were said to be disloyal. A group of "no, no" people and "yes, yes" people were brought together to iron out some of the feelings between the two groups. Pat and Lily supported those who volunteered for military service.

Before 1953 when the Walter-McCarran Act was passed over President Truman's veto, no one of Japanese ancestry who was born in Japan could become an American citizen. A few people had fought in World War I and had been given citizenship.   Other   Asian-Americans   were   equally discriminated against, Filipinos particularly.   Filipinos in significant numbers had served in the Navy for many years. Some Japanese-Americans also had served aboard Navy ships in World War I, but none were given American citizenship.

Pat said, "During the Depression years, the community organization in Los Angeles of which my father was president collected money for people in need so that help could be provided wherever it was needed.   It was a closely knit organization and certainly effective. I remember going to these big picnics where my father presided.   They often developed panels listing how much people had donated. That information would often push some people to give more money.

"During the war this activity was construed as meaning he was collecting money for the Japanese government. He was a community leader. He was a vice chair of the veterans of the Russo-Japanese war. These were men who formed a veterans group which had meaning to them."

Pat said, "Our parents were not able to become citizens. No Asians could become citizens as Europeans could after living in the US for five years and having no blemish on their records. This anti-Asian discrimination came about with the passage of the Oriental Exclusion Act in the latter part of the 19th Century.

"In 1953 my father could become a citizen and he did. We joined with other efforts to get the passage of the Walter-McCarran Act. President Truman vetoed the bill for a repeal but Congress overrode his veto. One of our colleagues, Mike Masaoka went to see Senator McCarran to convince him of the importance of overriding the veto.

"It took a lot of persuasion by several people to have Congressman Walter, who was from Pennsylvania and who had no Japanese-Americans in his jurisdiction, to support this legislation. He felt that in 1952 things should be different so he voted for the bill."

Lily added, "My parents changed their names to Tom and Mary when they became citizens. My mother called one day in 1953 and said, 'This is Mrs. Mary Arikawa.' She said she was now a US citizen and very proud of it."

Pat said, "My mother did not become a citizen. She felt her English was too poor and she'd gotten along well without English. She could speak Spanish quite well. She had needed Spanish in order to talk to many of the customers of the store they had. Almost all of them were Mexican, and most could not speak English, so you had to talk to them in their language which, of course, was Spanish. It was much easier to learn Spanish than English. Spanish has more similarities to the sounds found in Japanese. She saw no reason to go to school to learn things about the Constitution which she hadn't needed up to then."

"We lost customers at the store during the Depression. Most of the customers were Mexican. They paid only when they got their pay checks. When times got very bad, they were sent back to Mexico. The store went broke, and my parents then shifted to a flower shop. No more grocery store," Pat explained.

Pat also added, "My father was held for three years in various prisoner-of-war camps. He had been sent to a camp outside of Santa Fe, New Mexico. Plans were being made for him to be deported to Japan from Santa Fe. I felt I should go to Santa Fe to see if I could get this order changed.

"Father Flanagan did not want me to go. He thought I would get too mad. He said, 'Pat, your hot Irish temper will come out and you will only make matters worse.'

"I accepted his advice, and one of my brothers who was

in the US Army went to Santa Fe to testify before the Deportation Board. My father was released after three years of being interned and allowed to join the rest of my family at Camp Jerome. Lily and I were able to get the authorities to send him and other members of my family to Omaha. My father obtained a job at Boys Town working in the laundry."

Pat continued, "Many sad things happen to people during wartime. In 1944 my youngest brother was killed while he was in the US Army. The Army then wanted to send my other brother to be a replacement, but Father Flanagan again helped to get this order changed. Instead he was sent to Ft. Snelling, Minnesota.

"He found the people in Minnesota to be the most friendly and helpful people he had ever met. He was sent to the Military Language School to learn Japanese. The thought was that he could be an interrogator for the Pacific Theater of War. While he did learn some Japanese during the year in Minnesota and was sent to Japan to interrogate prisoners, he interrogated only 12 prisoners. He was attached to a Marine Unit where they soon recognized that he was a great baseball player so he played baseball all over Japan. He had been drafted in the Army in October 1941.

. "Some Japanese-Americans were deported to Japan when the father of the family was threatened with deportation. They lost their citizenship; but later Congress changed this decision and they were able to come back after the war. JACL was behind this effort."

Lily said, "My mother was sent to Arkansas. She was able to join my father in Crystal City, Texas, much later."

Pat said, "When we went to Japan after the war, I contacted some relatives there. There were about 13 of them whom we met, and they all had photographs. Many Issei's like my father would send pictures of their first-born to them.

I remember how many of these people said I looked so much like my father whom they had known. We were said to have dual citizenship, American and Japanese.

"Many of the older Japanese-Americans, especially the first-born, were registered in the family register in Japan.

"When war was declared in 1941, many of the Japanese-Americans were said to have dual citizenship because their names appeared in the family register in Japan. In most cases this fact was not known or respected by the Japanese-Americans born before World War II. I was required to declare later that I was not a citizen of Japan. To do so I was obliged to take out an ad in a newspaper where I said I renounced dual citizenship with Japan."

In his chapter entitled *The Perpetual Foreigner*, Professor Frank Wu describes the anguish experienced by Asian-American people who were decent, law-abiding people but who were constantly being discriminated against and shunned by Caucasian European-Americans.[1]

Finding a House in Omaha

"Soon we felt very much at home in Omaha. We both liked the work we were doing, and we enjoyed being a part of a community again. The midwestern people were friendly and helpful in most respects," Pat and Lily both said.

"After we had been at the campus of Boys Town for a few months, we talked to Father Flanagan to see about finding a house somewhere in Omaha so we could be even more a part of the community. Father Flanagan was agreeable and gave us the names of some Realtors who might be helpful. It was a difficult process as it turned out. The conversation would proceed something like this," Pat said.

The first call was to the Heritage Realty Company (a fictitious name).

"Hello, this is Mr. Pat Okura. May I speak to Mr. Brundage please?"

"This is Tom Brundage, what can I do for you?"

"My wife and I have recently moved to Omaha. We both have been working for Father Flanagan at Boys Town for several months, and we're now in the market for a house," Pat said.

"Of course. We have a number of houses. What did you have in mind?" Mr. Brundage replied.

"We were thinking of something modest, perhaps a three bed room house. Do you have anything of that variety?"

"Yes, indeed. We're always happy to help people who work with Father Flanagan. Why don't you and your wife come over to the office and I can show you what we have," Mr. Brundage said.

"That would be fine. When would be a good time?"

"How about Monday afternoon, say about 1 o'clock?"

"Yes, my wife, Lily, and I can be there. We heard about

some houses in north Omaha," Pat said.

"Oh yes, we have houses all over the city."

"We look forward to seeing you. My name is Pat Okura, O-k-u-r-a."

"All right, I'll put you down, Mr. O'Kura, for one o'clock on Monday," he said.

"When we went over to his office, we looked at several photographs of houses which were being listed by Heritage posted on the walls. One or two of them looked exactly like what we wanted. Mr. Brundage's receptionist went into his office to let him know we were in the waiting room."

"When Mr. Brundage came out of the office, he glanced first at me and then at Lily, but didn't smile at either of us," Pat said.

"Hello, Mr. and Mrs. Okura. You say you're working for Father Flanagan? We all admire the work which he is doing out there at Boys' Town. Please sit down," he said.

"We saw some pictures in your waiting room of several attractive houses," Pat said.

Having looked us over and decided that we were not Irish, we could almost hear doors closing. "Oh, I'm so sorry, this house was just taken off the market. It's too bad you didn't come in earlier. This one on Adams Street was sold only yesterday. You might do better to contact some of the other Realtors, perhaps in Bellevue," said Mr. Brundage.

They contacted three other Realtors and heard the same story. Houses were always just taken off the market, or they had been sold within the past few days.

About this time Pat answered a newspaper ad for an apartment. Before getting too far into the conversation with Mrs. Martin E. Lof, the wife of a local builder, originally from Sweden, Pat pointed out that Lily and he were Japanese-Americans. Mrs. Lof stated that this made no difference to them so they went to visit the second floor apartment. After their being rebuffed so many times, it was like a fresh breeze to encounter someone who was instantly helpful.

The Lofs had been renting the house from people who were then living in California. The apartment which the Okuras rented was in effect a sublet. Mr. Lof turned out to be a great friend indeed. He lent them a car to get around the city and when the time came to move in, he sent one of his construction company's trucks out to Boys Town to pick up their few belongings.

Pat and Lily became good friends with Mr. and Mrs. Lof. When it came time for them to build their own 'dream house,' it was Mr. Lof who built it for them in West Omaha. The Lofs were the type of people who were always helping others. During the war tires were rationed so that when Mr. Lof gave his ration coupon for tires to a man who was working at Boys Town, it was a big event.

The apartment rented to them by the Lofs was a great improvement over anything they had had so far. After living in the apartment for about a year, the actual owners of the apartment, who were still living in California, heard from neighbors that the Lofs had rented to a Japanese couple. They strenuously objected to having "Japs" in their house and they insisted that the Lofs remove Pat and Lily from their apartment. The Lofs expressed their deep disappointment to the Okuras for having again to see them sent out to hunt for another home. Fortunately they were able to find another apartment to rent.

After renting for another two years, they felt they were ready for a house of their own. After the fourth rebuff from Realtors, Pat decided to talk to Father Flanagan to see what he would suggest.

"Yes, that's right. Each time it was the same. Lily and I were always given a cordial invitation to come to the office, and then as soon as the agent saw that we were of Japanese descent, everything changed. I'm sure they thought I was Irish having misinterpreted our name. What do you suggest we might do? Father Flanagan scratched his head and then said, 'I'm not quite sure, Pat, but let me make some inquiries and see what I can do,' " Pat related.

In a few days Father Flanagan called Pat into his office and told him that another Realtor had been lined up in North Omaha. "He knows all about you, knows that you're Japanese-Americans, and he'll show you a couple of places which may be what you're looking for," he said.

Pat continued, "One of the houses proved to be exactly what we had in mind. We began the process of getting all of the financing taken care of which went well at one of the local banks. We went out to the house every night to look around. We began to think about what type of draperies would be suitable and where we would want to place furniture, all the things which young homeowners do. In about a week we encountered another road block."

"The section of town where this house was located was heavily populated by Catholics, and some of them on seeing us around the house thought that we might not be suitable neighbors, and so they began developing a petition to keep us from acquiring the house and moving in," Pat said.

Once again Pat turned to Father Flanagan to let him know what new developments were taking place.

"I'm sorry to bother you about our personal affairs again, Father, but it looks as though some of the neighbors in North Omaha are going to try to keep us out of the neighborhood. They are mostly Catholic people and I guess they fear our presence would be upsetting. They are developing some kind of petition to this effect. We had already moved some of our clothes and few possessions into the house. We didn't know what to expect next," Pat said.

"Oh, I think I can handle that one," Father Flanagan said with a bit of a twinkle in his eye.

"The next day was Sunday. All afternoon a series of different Catholic priests came to visit us. They were all very cordial. A new priest would arrive about every hour. We served them a bit of tea and talked about some of the things we were doing at Boys Town, and then they left. After each one left, they would often talk to some of the neighbors who seemed to pop out of their own houses to get some idea of what was going on. We never knew exactly what was said, but it seemed clear that a stamp of approval had been placed on us. In any event the efforts to develop a petition for our removal never went beyond the talking stage, so we moved in.

"Eventually we were accepted by our new neighbors, and some became good friends in time," Lily added.

The Early Years In Omaha

The 17 years with Father Flanagan at Boys Town were good years for both Pat and Lily. Aside from the Spencer Tracy movie on Father Flanagan and Boys Town, Pat and Lily had not known much about Boys Town. What they did know was that it was a way out of the camp at Santa Anita and a chance to start over. For Pat, especially, it meant an opportunity to use his skills as a psychologist once again.

Boys Town had been founded in 1917 in a small facility, located at 19th Street and Dodge Street in downtown Omaha, serving five youngsters. At first the program grew slowly, but with the increased number of boys additional space was required. In 1929 Boys Town acquired 250 acres, well beyond the western city limits on West Dodge Road.

Throughout the Depression years, however, the growth was sporadic as money from any source came in slowly. Father Flanagan wanted the funds to come from various sources but not from the Catholic Church. After the Spencer Tracy film on Father Flanagan and Boys Town, which was produced in 1937, more funds came into Boys Town as its fame spread. When Pat and Lily arrived in 1942 , there were 450 boys. By 1959 the number of boys at Boys Town had grown to 1,000, and the number of employees had increased to about 250. These employees consisted of teachers, building and grounds personnel, dairy workers, food service personnel and many others.

One of the cardinal principles of Boys Town was its emphasis on helping everyone to acquire a usable skill. Some of the boys would eventually become professional people in medicine and the law, for example, but everyone was helped to have a marketable skill, with the emphasis on vocational training in order to be able to work in laundries, barber shops, catering services, ceramics making, bakeries, etc.

A system of government was set up so that a different boy would be elected mayor of Boys Town each year. Not only did these young boys come to know something about the civic responsibilities involved in such offices, but they also experienced being given new and much needed respect from their associates and also from the adults of the organization who were serving as their role models.

A major concern always for Father Flanagan was that these delinquent boys should have a second chance. They had come to delinquency through no fault of their own. The only weapon they had learned was how to fight back. Father Flanagan insisted that by providing them with good role models, love, respect and intensive work programs, he could change these boys. He often would state with confidence, "There is no such thing as a bad boy." The boys would usually spend three to seven years at the facility and graduate to a regular job or to go on to higher education.

Some people criticized Father Flanagan for not having enough social workers in his program to assist in the efforts to rehabilitate these boys. Eventually as funds became available, more social workers and other staff were added.

Since Father Flanagan was always interested and concerned with helping people who were not doing well in the society at large for whatever reason, he thought there might be an opportunity to help some of the Japanese-Americans in California being interned in the assembly centers. He contacted the Maryknoll Fathers in California to see if any Japanese-Americans would be willing to come to Boys Town. In turn the Fathers contacted the Archdiocese of Los Angeles to see if this plan could be effected.

Six families identified by Pat and Lily came to Boys Town from the Santa Anita Assembly Center as a result of the interventions by Lily's boss at Santa Anita, Mr. England.

One of these men had a degree in agriculture and was placed in charge of the 500-acre farm. Pat and Lily were the last of the group to arrive.

Pat was the first psychologist ever at Boys Town. Much later a psychiatrist was added to the program. Pat was assigned to test many of the boys and he most likely administered thousands of different psychological tests to the clientele at Boys Town. He estimated that he probably conducted over 5,000 IQ tests during his 17 years there.

Because he was adept at identifying the type of boy who would probably benefit from the program at Boys Town, Pat was soon asked to assist with the screening of applicants for admission as the number of applicants from around the country continued to grow.

Few agencies concerned with delinquent youth were willing to take African-Americans, Asian-Americans, or Hispanic-Americans. Father Flanagan was willing to accept boys from any minority group. The boys' religious preferences made no difference in the application process.

Many people from the US and other countries visited Boys Town. For example, in 1947 the Minister of Welfare from Japan came to see Boys Town to determine if they could incorporate some of Father Flanagan's ideas to comparable situations in Japan.

Pat spoke of Father Flanagan as "a powerful person who was an excellent speaker. He was a very out-going man who warmed up quickly to people and they to him." Father Flanagan had many requests to make presentations to all manner of organizations. Sometimes he would ask Pat to pinch hit for him when the demand was too great or there were conflicting dates. Having this opportunity helped Pat to become better acquainted with many communities not only across Nebraska but also in many places in the Middle West.

During these years at Boys Town, Pat became active in the Urban League in Omaha and later became president of the Nebraska Chapter. In this connection he was frequently asked to mediate in the African-American community. At one point the FBI asked Pat why he was so friendly with the African-Americans.

The answer seemed natural to Pat. Helping others with their problems involving civil rights was just an extension of the work to which he had been dedicating himself with the Japanese-American community.

After World War II had ended, new social issues arose. Father Flanagan was asked by the War Department to go to Germany to offer some advice on what to do with German orphans. While he was in Berlin, he suffered a fatal heart attack and died in 1948.

Father Flanagan had groomed Father Walsh to be his successor. Father Walsh had attended Catholic University in Washington, D.C. where he had obtained a master's degree in social work. A charismatic type, he liked making contact with communities and gave talks wherever asked.

However, Bishop Ryan, who was bishop of the Diocese of Omaha at the time, selected Monsignor Wegner to be the new director of Boys Town. Msgr. Wegner did not like public appearances. In many ways he seemed to Pat to be so different from Father Flanagan. Msgr. Wegner was a great scholar, and he also had been in charge of an orphanage in Omaha. Father Walsh became a parish priest in Omaha and died in his fifties.

Pat was devoted to Boys Town and all that it stood for as an important facility dedicated to helping delinquent boys. After being there for 17 years, a new opportunity presented itself.

Later Years in Omaha

In 1959 Pat left Boys Town to accept a newly established position as Chief Probation Officer in the Juvenile Court System of Douglas County, the county in which Omaha is located.

Up to this point, juveniles were handled by the adult court system and were placed in adult jails. The injustices of this approach seem obvious now, but at that time many states had no special provisions for juvenile offenders. From his work at Boys Town Pat was all too aware of how a jail experience for a young boy would add insult to an already injured person. Rehabilitation efforts became much more difficult for a youngster who had been traumatized by being incarcerated with hardened criminals.

Pat had been active in trying to get a separate court system established for juveniles. In the process of this work he became involved in many communities in an effort to upgrade the background of persons who were doing work in child welfare. In time he became one of the best informed persons in the state about the extent and variety of the issues, not only for young adolescents but adults as well.

The requirements in many states for becoming a child welfare worker were not well defined. The job was often arduous and some of the county workers with were ill prepared to accept these positions. Some of the workers would be on call seven days a week.

Catholic University in Washington, DC had been helpful in setting up a program for the training of persons who were doing child welfare work. Initially the program was for only one year but later Catholic University and other schools increased the training time to two years.

Gradually some of Pat's interests started to shift as he

began learning more about the state system and was advising about how the child welfare programs could be strengthened throughout the state. In the early days of the Kennedy administration legislation had been passed to develop state wide planning in all aspects of mental health. Pat was asked to head up this effort in Nebraska. The proposals which emerged from this planning effort became the Mental Health Plan for Nebraska. The plan was well conceived, comprehensive and all inclusive. It served the state well for the next several years.

In 1963 Pat took a position at the Nebraska Psychiatric Institute of the University of Nebraska College of Medicine, working under the direction of Dr. Cecil Wittson who was the Director of the Nebraska Psychiatric Institute and Chairman of the Department of Psychiatry of the University of Nebraska College of Medicine.

The Nebraska Psychiatric Institute was founded with the concept that in the future the needs of persons with various mental health problems would increasingly be solved in conjunction with community-based programs and activities.

Pat's knowledge and experience throughout the state was well suited and invaluable in this position where more and more emphasis on community mental health programs was taking form as opposed to the long term hospitalization which had been the main form of care in Nebraska as well as other states. He now was much less occupied with hands on help for individual children but became involved in helping to establish policy in the many areas of mental health. One of the activities which he was instrumental in initiating was with establishing various programs for delinquent girls. For a long time people had the belief that only boys became delinquent which certainly is not valid.

Always active in the Japanese American Citizens League

(JACL), Pat became even more involved in 1963 in some of the Civil Rights activities which were then becoming increasingly prominent in the country. Pat had served progressively as third vice president, second vice president, first vice president and eventually as president of JACL. In all of these positions Pat fostered the development of many more chapters throughout the country. By 1963 there were over 100 chapters of JACL in the country.

As Civil Rights issues became more prominent in the affairs of the country, many members and officers of JACL were opposed to becoming involved with any plans for greater involvement with the African-American community. Essentially many felt that the issues for African Americans were different than those which the Japanese Americans had to confront.

Pat was a leader in the discussion about what the status of JACL should be with reference to the Civil Rights programs and the need to support African Americans as another minority group wherever possible.

The March on Washington being organized by Dr. Martin Luther King, Jr. created a sharp divide in JACL. Pat, who was the national president at the time was determined that JACL should participate in the march. He called a special board meeting in Omaha to hammer out an accord on issues of civil rights. Eventually Pat as President of JACL and 50 other members from around the country agreed to participate in the March.

Those who opposed to participating in the march stated that the issues of African Americans were their business, their problem and that JACL should not become involved.[1] However, Pat felt differently. He said, "I was for this area of Civil Rights." He was very proud to march side by side with Dr. Martin Luther King, Jr.

In the meantime Lily was certainly not idle. After working at Boys Town Welfare Department for two years, Lily and Pat were befriended by Ruth M. Campbell, Executive Director of the YWCA in Omaha. She was instrumental in assisting the Okuras in establishing a Japanese American Citizens League Chapter and was willing to have YWCA facilities used for JACL meetings.

Through this friendship, Lily was asked to become her secretary at the YWCA. In this capacity during the 1940's she had an opportunity to use her skills and background to take on progressively more responsibility as office manager, building manager, and later as Acting Director of the YWCA.

As a result of these experiences, Lily was asked to join the National Secretaries Association. On the local level she served on the Board and then became the Omaha Chapter President. In 1956 she became the first Japanese American to be elected International Vice President, representing all of the chapters in the northwest region.

Ever ready to take on more responsibilities, Lily served on the Board of Directors of JACL from 1956-1960 and again from 1963-1968. She was elected Governor of the Mountain Plains District Council.

Her considerable talents for organizing and directing were quickly recognized in another situation. The University Hospital of the University of Nebraska Medical Center had just hired a new director who was eager to have a highly qualified person as his assistant.

One day he called Lily to see if she would be interested. At first Lily did not want to move from her present position at the YWCA, but Mr. Johnson was very persuasive. He invited her to come to see the hospital and to tell her something of his plans for her. Finally she accepted in 1946 after a few weeks of negotiations.

While employed by the University of Nebraska Medical Center, Lily was approached by the Building and Planning Committee of the Board of Directors of what became the C. Louis Meyer Therapy Center. At this time the center was a private and independent unit on the University of Nebraska Medical Center campus. She was asked to coordinate the planning, including the financial planning for that center.

In order to take this position she left the University Hospital in 1957 and established an office in the Medical Building just off the campus of the Medical Center. In this new capacity she was responsible to the Hill-Burton staff in Washington and the Regional Office in maintaining accurate financial records during the building period.

She was also responsible to a Board of 33 members. It was necessary to establish policies and procedures for over 50 employees. In addition she set up training courses for nursing students in the field of rehabilitation in cooperation with Childrens Memorial Hospital, located less than a block from the Meyer Therapy Center.

Once the building was completed, Lily was asked to be the Administrator and Coordinator of the Meyer Therapy Center for Children, which was affiliated with the University of Nebraska Medical Center. The Meyer Center provided coordinated medical and other health related services to children with various disabilities. Lily continued in this position until 1968.

Dr. Cecil Wittson who had now become the Chancellor of the Medical Center was interested in establishing a volunteer program at the medical center. Dr. Wittson asked Mr. Richard Schripsema, the Hospital Director, to sound out what interest Lily might have in assuming this new position. She accepted the challenge and began recruiting volunteers through the Faculty Wives Club and other community organizations.

One of Dr. Wittson's special interests was the gift shop in the new University Hospital. He asked Lily to assume this responsibility directly. Lily felt it was a particular privilege to use her talents to design the Gift Shop and attend to all aspects of the purchasing. In addition to organizing the adult volunteers, she also developed a teen aged group of young people called the Volunteens. She enjoyed this new experience very much and she soon made the Hospital Gift Shop an outstanding facility. This experience added to her store house of talents. Some of the proceeds of the Gift Shop were used to purchase an ambulance to pick up patients who were flown in from out state places such as Grand Island and Scottsbluff.

Among her other community activities Lily was deeply involved in the Altrusa Club, an organization for business and professional women. The name Altrusa is a derivation of altruism, defined as the principle or practice of unselfish concern for or a devotion to the welfare of others. Altrusa International is a worldwide service association of business and professional people united in personal development and fellowship.

Working together in local clubs, members volunteer their time, energies and expertise in a wide variety of projects dedicated to community improvements. Drawing upon the leadership, abilities, talents, and altruistic motivations of its members, Altrusans seek to make their combined services more effective on the local, national and international levels. While in Omaha, Lily was elected to the Board of Directors and in 1963 she was elected President of the Omaha Club.

From their early days in Omaha onward both Pat and Lily dreamed of one day building their own house, their dream house. Now in the late 50's they were in a position to do so. They contracted their friend Mr. Lof who worked with them to design and then build a house which incorporated both Japanese and American features. It was charming and practical. As part of their plan they developed a garden which incorporated many features which one would find in Japan. House and home became a showplace in the Omaha community. Both Pat and Lily loved to entertain their many friends. One of their delights was to have a traditional Japanese dinner on New Years Eve. All of the dinner, including the sushi, Lily would prepare herself. To be invited to this dinner was a rare treat.

The Years in Washington

While living in Omaha, Pat had often made applications for various federal positions but he was never accepted. A form letter would come back stating that he was 'ineligible.' Consequently when the offer came to become associated with the National Institute of Mental Health (NIMH) in Bethesda, Pat at first was wary about accepting a position with the federal government. The memories of how the federal government had been responsible for uprooting and incarcerating all of his family and all of his people were deeply etched in his memory.

In time the director of NIMH, Dr. Bertram Brown, persuaded him that there were opportunities in community mental health programs which needed to be developed across the country. Dr. Brown had told Pat that he was interested in fostering three programs in NIMH which were developing and expanding community mental health programs, improving mental health services for children, and helping more minorities find careers in mental health. Since these were matters about which Pat was greatly interested, he agreed in 1971 to go to Washington on a trial basis. Lily would remain in Omaha until a final decision was made.

The new position as Executive Assistant to the Director required extensive travel. By carefully scheduling his travel, Pat was able to return to Omaha almost every weekend. Towards the end of the first year Pat, convinced that this new position offered him new and challenging opportunities, decided to make the move permanent.

Leaving Omaha was a wrench for both but especially Lily since she had become very successful in her latest position as Director of Volunteers of the new University Hospital gift shop as well as all of the several volunteer programs. Selling their home with its wonderful garden, which had developed into a showplace of Asian design, was also difficult. There were many memories of home past and present which would have to be transported to a new place with many unknown aspects to consider. Only people who have weathered the upheaval of a move after living in a community for a quarter of a century can appreciate how difficult a change of this sort can be.

Being executive assistant to a dynamic person such as Dr. Bert Brown was challenging from the start. Pat was given broad responsibilities to help in the development of grants to the states to develop new initiatives in providing community mental health services. With the advent of new medications such as thorazine it was now possible to help patients who had spent many years in mental institutions to gain a new life in a community.

To be successful there was a need to establish strong community support. Because the idea of providing community based services to person with various types of mental illness was a difficult concept for many to accept, Pat, with the s strong support of Dr. Brown, was able to help the states to move in that direction.

Dr. Brown would have daily meetings with the directors of research, training and community services. During some of these sessions, it became clear that there was need to have greater contact with the several state administrations. Pat was given the task of setting up talks for Dr. Brown which he would accept as long as there was an opportunity to meet with the governor for at least 30 minutes. He made this request so that he could try to persuade the chief executive of the state to foster some of the programs in which NIMH had an interest, but especially those having to do with community mental health.

Much sought after as a speaker at scientific meetings, Pat was asked by many organizations to speak about contemporary issues in mental health. Beginning in 1973 he spoke to well over 25 groups throughout the United States but also to international groups in Europe and Asia. The range of topics included discussions of how mental health services should be expanded in local communities and in the states, the current status of Asian American race relationships and the vast need to expand and improve the mental health services available for children and youth.

Meanwhile in 1946 a Washington Chapter of JACL had been established. As this chapter grew, it attracted the attention not only of Japanese-Americans but also Jewish and African-American groups who lent their support. As a result of pressure from JACL, Congress in 1980 established a commission to study the internment of Japanese-Americans and their families. The report, Personal Justice Denied concluded, "The record does not permit the conclusion that military necessity warranted the exclusion of ethnic Japanese from the West Coast."[1]

All of this renewed interest in the World War II internment of Japanese-American persons was used to obtain the passage of the Civil Liberties Act in 1988. In turn this led to the Reparations Act (1990) which provided $ 20,000 to each Japanese American person who had been interned in an Assembly Center or a Relocation Camp. Many other Civil Rights Organization helped in obtaining this apology 60 years later.

When the letters of apology first came out from the White House, plain stationery without any heading was used. Many people protested to such an extent that President George H. W. Bush was persuaded to reissue the letters using official White House stationery. (Fig. 3) Pat served as

Executive Assistant to the Director of NIMH from 1970 to 1985. Dr. Brown was having some personnel differences with Secretary Califano which resulted in his being made an Assistant Secretary for Health but he no longer had any direct line responsibilities. Dr. Brown left NIMH in 1985 to become President of Hahneman University in Philadelphia and Pat continued to do some work for Dr. Brown until 1987 when he retired.

When asked to comment about the Okuras for this book Dr. Brown said, "As you know I am more than just a friend. I have admired them and been inspired by their courage, commitment and contributions." 2

When Lily moved to Washington she had hoped to take a year to settle in to the new surroundings and to decorate their new home. With her background it was not surprising that within a month she was asked by the Director of Public Affairs of the Corporation for Public Broadcasting to become his secretary. He especially wanted someone of Asian American background. She told him that she was not seeking a position at this time and that her experiences were beyond that of a secretarial level. When he learned about her background, he suggested that she should send in a resume to Mr. John Golden, the Vice President.

She did not expect to hear from Mr. Golden but she did send her resume to him. Surprisingly she heard from him within two days. Although she was at first reluctant to take on something in an organization about which she had little information, she did accept the position as Director of Personnel Services.

This position was a new one which she was able to design from top to bottom. She devised and incorporated new and more effective ways of tracking applications of people who were seeking employment with the agency. This step was only one of several things which she did to improve and streamline the organization. Lily continued in this position for ten years.

Once the decision was made to move permanently to Washington, Lily was soon continuing her involvement in many community activities. She was elected to the Board of Directors of the Washington Chapter of the Japanese American Citizen League from 1973 to 1975. Previously she had been active in Altrusa programs in Omaha and she was soon involved in similar ones in Washington. In 1979 she became President of the Altrusa Club of Washington, DC. In addition she headed the Personnel Committee of the YWCA of the National Capital Area.

When Lily finally retired in 1982 from some of these activities, she became interested in the art of dressing Japanese dolls which are called kimekomi. The fashioning of these dolls with their intricate clothing required her to take a special course in order to become a certified instructor.

Pleased with this accomplishment, she was now able to become a teacher. She now teaches about three or four women at a time in this ancient art of Japanese doll making. Because of the fine and tedious work required, it takes about three months to complete a doll. At their home Lily has several examples of these magnificent dolls which she has exhibited at their church and in various schools. Among her other activities in her retirement Lily has been editing the Washington, DC Japanese American Citizens League (JACL) newsletter.

Both Pat and Lily have continued their long interest in and support of the Presbyterian Church. Between the two of them they have served as deacons, elders and they have served on many church committees. The Pastor of their church, the Bradley Hills Presbyterian Churc in Bethesda,

Dr. Susan Andrews, at a banquet honoring Pat on his 90th birthday, said, "We have much to learn from the Okuras about how to live."[3]   Most people who know them would agree.

Pat Okura with his parents, 1912

The Arikawa family, Lily on left, 1923

Lily Arikawa, Nisei week, 1937

Pat Okura (extreme left) with his father and four brothers,
circa 1932

Pat Okura and Father Flanagan, 1943

Pat and Lily Okura, Senator Inouye and President Kennedy, 1962

Pat Okura and Dr. Bert Brown at National Institute of
Mental Health, circa 1980

Pat and Lily Okura, Christmas 2003

AUTHORIZING THE SECRETARY OF WAR TO
PRESCRIBE MILITARY AREAS

WHEREAS the successful prosecution
of the war requires every possible protection against espionage and against

sabotage to national-defense material,
national-defense premises, and national-defense utilities as defined in Section
4, Act of April 20, 1918, 40 Stat. 533, as
amended by the Act of November 30,
1940, 54 Stat. 1220, and the Act of Au-
gust 21, 1941, 55 Stat. 655 (U.S.C., Title
50, Sec. 104):

NOW, THEREFORE, by virtue of the
authority vested in me as President of
the United States, and Commander in
Chief of the Army and Navy, I hereby
authorize and direct the Secretary of
War, and the Military Commanders
whom he may from time to time desig-
nate, whenever he or any designated
Commander deems such action necessary or desirable, to prescribe military
areas in such places and of such extent
as he or the appropriate Military Commander may determine, from which any
or all persons may be excluded, and with
respect to which, the right of any person
to enter, remain in, or leave shall be
subject to whatever restrictions the Secretary of War or the appropriate Military Commander may impose in his dis-
cretion. The Secretary of War is hereby
authorized to provide for residents of
any such area who are excluded there-
from, such transportation, food, shelter,
and other accommodations as may be
necessary, in the judgment of the Secretary of War or the said Military Commander, and until other arrangements
are made, to accomplish the purpose of
this order. The designation of military
areas in any region or locality shall supersede designations of prohibited and
restricted areas by the Attorney General
under the Proclamations of December 7
and 8, 1941, and shall supersede the responsibility and authority of the Attorney General under the said Proclamations in respect of such prohibited and
restricted areas.

I hereby further authorize and direct
the Secretary of War and the said Military Commanders to take such other
steps as he or the appropriate Military
Commander may deem advisable to en-
force compliance with the restrictions
applicable to each Military area herein-
above authorized to be designated, including the use of Federal troops and
other Federal Agencies, with authority
to accept assistance of state and local
agencies.

I hereby further authorize and direct
all Executive Departments, independent
establishments and other Federal Agen-

cies, to assist the Secretary of War or
the said Military Commanders in carry-
ing out this Executive Order, including
the furnishing of medical aid, hospitalization, food, clothing, transportation,
use of land, shelter, and other supplies,
equipment, utilities, facilities, and services.

This order shall not be construed as
modifying or limiting in any way the
authority heretofore granted under Executive Order No. 8972, dated December
12, 1941, nor shall it be construed as limiting or modifying the duty and responsibility of the Federal Bureau of Investigation, with respect to the investigation
of alleged acts of sabotage or the duty
and responsibility of the Attorney General and the Department of Justice under the Proclamations of December 7
and 8, 1941, prescribing regulations for
the conduct and control of alien ene-
mies, except as such duty and responsibility is superseded by the designation of
military areas hereunder.

FRANKLIN D ROOSEVELT

THE WHITE HOUSE,
February 19, 1942.

EXECUTIVE ORDER 9067

PROVIDING FOR THE TRANSFER OF
PERSONNEL TO WAR AGENCIES

By virtue of the authority vested in me
by the Civil Service Act (22 Stat. 403),
and by Section 1753 of the Revised Stat-
utes of the United States (U.S.C., title 5,
sec. 631), and in order to expedite the
transfer of personnel to war agencies,
it is hereby ordered as follows:

1. For the purpose of facilitating
transfers of employees under the provisions of this Order, the Director of the
Bureau of the Budget shall from time to
time establish priority classifications of
the several Executive departments and
agencies, or of parts or activities thereof,
in respect to their relative importance
to the war program, and such classifications shall be controlling as to transfers
under the provisions of this Order.

2. The Civil Service Commission is authorized to secure information as to employees of Executive departments and
agencies who are deemed competent to
perform essential war work in departments or agencies having a higher priority classification, and, with the consent

Figure 1 - Executive order No. 9066, signed by
President Franklin Roosevelt, Feb. 19, 1942

Civilian Exclusion Order No. 5

WESTERN DEFENSE COMMAND AND FOURTH ARMY
WARTIME CIVIL CONTROL ADMINISTRATION
Presidio of San Francisco, California
April 1, 1942

INSTRUCTIONS
TO ALL PERSONS OF
JAPANESE
ANCESTRY
LIVING IN THE FOLLOWING AREA:

All that portion of the City and County of San Francisco, State of California, lying generally west of the north-south line established by Junipero Serra Boulevard, Worchester Avenue, and Nineteenth Avenue, and lying generally north of the east-west line established by California Street, to the intersection of Market Street, and thence on Market Street to San Francisco Bay.

All Japanese persons, both alien and non-alien, will be evacuated from the above designated area by 12:00 o'clock noon, Tuesday, April 7, 1942.

No Japanese person will be permitted to enter or leave the above described area after 8:00 a. m., Thursday, April 2, 1942, without obtaining special permission from the Provost Marshal at the Civil Control Station located at:

1701 Van Ness Avenue
San Francisco, California

The Civil Control Station is equipped to assist the Japanese population affected by this evacuation in the following ways:

1. Give advice and instructions on the evacuation.

2. Provide services with respect to the management, leasing, sale, storage or other disposition of most kinds of property including: real estate, business and professional equipment, buildings, household goods, boats, automobiles, livestock, etc.

3. Provide temporary residence elsewhere for all Japanese in family groups.

4. Transport persons and a limited amount of clothing and equipment to their new residence, as specified below.

(OVER)

THE FOLLOWING INSTRUCTIONS MUST BE OBSERVED:

1. A responsible member of each family, preferably the head of the family, or the person in whose name most of the property is held, and each individual living alone, will report to the Civil Control Station to receive further instructions. This must be done between 8:00 a. m. and 5:00 p. m., Thursday, April 2, 1942, or between 8:00 a. m. and 5:00 p. m., Friday, April 3, 1942.

2. Evacuees must carry with them on departure for the Reception Center, the following property:

(a) Bedding and linens (no mattress) for each member of the family;

(b) Toilet articles for each member of the family;

(c) Extra clothing for each member of the family;

(d) Sufficient knives, forks, spoons, plates, bowls and cups for each member of the family;

(e) Essential personal effects for each member of the family.

All items carried will be securely packaged, tied and plainly marked with the name of the owner and numbered in accordance with instructions received at the Civil Control Station.

The size and number of packages is limited to that which can be carried by the individual or family group.

No contraband items as described in paragraph 6, Public Proclamation No. 3, Headquarters Western Defense Command and Fourth Army, dated March 24, 1942, will be carried.

3. The United States Government through its agencies will provide for the storage at the sole risk of the owner of the more substantial household items, such as iceboxes, washing machines, pianos and other heavy furniture. Cooking utensils and other small items will be accepted if crated, packed and plainly marked with the name and address of the owner. Only one name and address will be used by a given family.

4. Each family, and individual living alone, will be furnished transportation to the Reception Center. Private means of transportation will not be utilized. All instructions pertaining to the movement will be obtained at the Civil Control Station.

Go to the Civil Control Station at 1701 Van Ness Avenue, San Francisco, California, between 8:00 a. m. and 5:00 p. m. Thursday, April 2, 1942, or between 8:00 a. m. and 5:00 p. m., Friday, April 3, 1942, to receive further instructions.

J. L. DeWITT
Lieutenant General, U. S. Army
Commanding

See Civilian Exclusion Order No. 5

Figure 2 - Notice for Evacuation

THE WHITE HOUSE

WASHINGTON

A monetary sum and words alone cannot restore lost years or erase painful memories; neither can they fully convey our Nation's resolve to rectify injustice and to uphold the rights of individuals. We can never fully right the wrongs of the past. But we can take a clear stand for justice and recognize that serious injustices were done to Japanese Americans during World War II.

In enacting a law calling for restitution and offering a sincere apology, your fellow Americans have, in a very real sense, renewed their traditional commitment to the ideals of freedom, equality, and justice. You and your family have our best wishes for the future.

Sincerely,

[signature: G. Bush]

United States Treasury 15-51 M 029,574,947

Check No.

10 10 90 02 WASHINGTON, D.C.   3007 23071093

008150942   M2   JUSTICE LG 0001M01008 15010004

Pay to the order of

K PATRICK OKURA
6303 FRIENDSHIP COURT $**20000*00
BETHESDA   MD 20817   VOID AFTER ONE YEAR

PER ENCLOSED MAILING NOTICE

30074   :000000518: 23071093 1: 011090

Figure 3 - Reparation letter from President G. H. W. Bush
and Check facsimile

Establishing the Okura Foundation

Many Japanese American people continue to follow an old tradition around their 77th birthday. The concept has always been to take stock of one's accomplishments and to decide if there is a further step to be taken to make a contribution to the world in which one finds himself.

After the reparation fund of $ 20,000 per person had been distributed (Figure 3), Pat and Lily conceived the idea of establishing a Foundation with their money. In addition to the $ 40,000 which they received from the government they added an equal amount from their own savings and the Okura Mental Health Foundation was born.

A formal announcement was made at Pat's 77th birthday party on October 1, 1988 at the Lakewood Country Club in Rockville, Maryland. Friends and relatives from the area as well as well as from many places around the country came to wish Pat well on this momentous occasion and to learn what this new Foundation would attempt to offer.

The purposes of the Okura Mental Health Foundation are:
"1. To foster and promote

a) education, research and services in the areas of mental health and human services, and

b) leadership by providing fellowships, scholarships, stipends and grants from promising Asian Pacific American professionals, students and relevant and related organizations.
2. To support and conduct activities, meetings, conferences, symposia, publications and related activities to

a) stimulate Asian Pacific Americans to enter the mental health and human services fields and

b) pursue and assume national and international leadership roles.

3. To engage in any lawful activities
  a) incidental to the foregoing purposes and
  b) appropriate to an organization which is exempt under
501 (C)(3) status of the Internal Revenue Services Code."

Some Japanese Americans have been unable to put all of
those unpleasant memories behind them. Many will not talk
at all about their internment and all of the heartbreak which
that war time situation engendered. Both Pat and Lily have
said repeatedly that their bitterness about the way they and
their families in the Japanese American community had been
treated in 1942, was now gone. It was time to turn
disappointment into a positive feature.

They decided that it would be important to offer young
Asian Pacific American students opportunities to enlarge
their scope of understanding about mental health issues.
Promoting their ideas by way of providing scholarships for
these students now became a primary activity for both Pat
and Lily. Pat as President of the Foundation and Lily as
Executive Director became a dynamic duo, and were
determined to make a success of this new organization. Over
ten years there have been over 90 young professionals who
have profited from these scholarships.

In September 1999 Pat celebrated his 88th birthday with
another party given at the Ft. Myer Officers Club in
Arlington, Virginia. The donations from this party would be
added to the Foundation as they had done in the past. In a
decade this Foundation had established itself as a significant
force in helping young Asian Pacific American professional
workers to grasp some of the complexities of how
government works and how objectives at the community level
can be accomplished. Many of the Fellows have attained
advancements in their chosen fields and have furthered their
endeavors by leadership training provided by the Okura

Foundation.

In addition to the regular fellowship program there have now been three persons who have gone on to spend a year as a White House Fellow. Being a White House Fellow provides an intensive look at the federal government. They learn more details about the ways in which laws are forged and eventually implemented.

One of the highlights of the program has been a 'Week in Washington' where these future leaders learn ways to build on their past knowledge and experience to enable them to assume leadership roles their respective communities both nationally and locally.

During this time they will have opportunities to meet members of Congress, officials in the Department of Health and Human Service, and staff members in the National Institutes of Health. The emphasis is on learning and comprehending how the system works in the complex organizational maze of the federal government in Washington and its many branches in the states and local communities.

Such basic concepts as how laws are made, how they progress through the various committee structures of Congress and how they are implemented once they become law are part of what these fellows will come to understand as a result of the contacts in Washington. Although some of the Japanese Americans who were interned, refuse to talk about that episode in their lives, the Okuras, on the other hand, point out to these young professionals how one keeps on working to correct adversity and one does not submit to its crushing effect on the lives of the people.

As a tribute to Pat's efforts to foster United States and Japanese Mental Health relations, he was given an award by the Japanese government, the Order of the Rising Sun, in a ceremony on December 13, 1999. The presentation was made by the Ambassador to the United States from Japan, Mr. Shunji Yanai. The tribute read in part:

"This evening is both a meaningful and joyous occasion. And I'm delighted so many friends of Mr. Okura's could be with us to help him celebrate his well-deserved recognition.

"We are here to present an honor to a remarkable man. In thinking what I should say about Mr. Okura, I asked myself why has this man accomplished so much? Why has he dedicated himself, throughout his life, to large and humane endeavors?

"I think that those are important questions for us to consider. I saw a quote the other day that I rather liked. It said, 'Adversity introduces a man to himself.' I believe the meaning has to do with how a person responds when confronted with adversity.

"Mr. Okura has seen adversity firsthand. In December 1941, two months after he and his wife, Lily, were married, they were packed off to a racetrack in Santa Anita, California, where they slept on straw mattresses on the floor. They lived in a stable for nine months.

"At UCLA, he was not allowed to live in the area where the university was located. He had to live elsewhere and to hitch-hike eight miles to the school every day.

"Also, at UCLA, he became the first Asian American to play and letter in a major sport at a West Coast college. He did this in the face of hostility and discrimination.

"I could give other examples. And what did he do when confronted with such adversity? To refer the quote, how was he introduced to himself?

"He responded to adversity by going into a field of work that seeks to understand and to heal. He went into psychology and mental health. He went into a field that calls upon one to give to others.

"He says that he learned about compassion from his father who visited the sick, handled funeral arrangements for families and in other ways served the people of his community.

"A book entitled, ***Remaking America***, devotes a whole chapter to Mr. Okura.[1] The book says of him, 'It was family honor and family respect that provided the moral underpinnings of Okura's urge to reach out and help others.'

"Reach out and help, he did. He has served the cause of mental health through his life's work and through the foundation that he established. He has served the cause of Japanese-American understanding. He has furthered the cause of justice and civil rights by his moral example. He has raised the status and visibility of Japanese-Americans and strengthened Japan-US relations.

"He has worked, to use the American phrase, 'for the greater good.'

"Mr. Okura, on behalf of both the Japanese present and the Americans present, I thank you for your life's work and for the greater good you have contributed to both our societies. And I would now like to present the award by reading a translation of the official decoration:

" 'The Order of the Rising Sun, Gold Rays with Rosette is hereby conferred upon Kiyoshi Patrick Okura, Citizen of the United States of America, by His Majesty the Emperor of Japan.

"In witness thereof, the Seal of State has been affixed to these present at the Imperial Palace. This Day, the Third of the Eleventh Month of the Eleventh Year of Heisei (1999).'

"And it is signed by the Prime Minister.

"On behalf of the Emperor, I present this decoration to .Mr. Okura... congratulations."

The story for the Okuras never ends. One of their latest

activities has been to work with many other Japanese Americans to establish a Memorial to Patriotism in Washington. The National Park Service provided a tract of land at the corner of Louisiana Avenue and First Street, NW in downtown Washington. The offer of the land was contingent on raising the necessary funds to erect the memorial. Over $ 8.5 million were raised to pay for its construction.

The memorial itself consists of two cranes striving to be free, which in turn are surrounded by barbed wire. It was a somber time for all who attended, including Pat and Lily as they looked at the inscriptions of the names of those who had died in service to their country, including the name of Pat's youngest brother. The dedication of the Memorial was November 9, 2000.

Attending the dedication were over 2,000 people, some of whom had served in World War II and many of whom were imprisoned in one or another of the 10 internment camps. Attorney General Janet Reno, the key speaker at the ceremonies, read a letter from President Clinton, which stated in part, "We are diminished when any American is targeted unfairly because of his or her heritage. This memorial and the internment sites are powerful reminders that stereotyping, discrimination, hatred, and racism have no place in the country."[2]

The Attorney General added, "This nation is at a moment in its history that will be recorded in the history books for years to come. It is a great nation because we have learned from our mistakes." [3]

Prejudice and discrimination do not end quickly.
Recently, February 9, 2003, two representatives from North Carolina, Howard Coble of Greensboro and Sue Myrick of Charlotte were criticized for insensitive remarks.

On a recent Washington talk show Coble said he believed President Roosevelt was right to send Japanese-Americans to internment camps during World War II. He said that this decision protected Japanese-Americans from a fearful, often intolerant public. He said, "Some [Japanese-Americans] probably were intent on doing harm to us. Just as some of these Arab-Americans are probably intent on doing harm to us."

Myrick, in a recent talk on domestic terrorism, referred to Arab-Americans and said, "Look who runs all the convenience stores across the country."

Three Asian-American members of Congress, Representatives Robert Matsui and Mike Honda California and David Wu of Oregon requested a meeting. In a letter they said, "Incarcerating citizens and legal resident aliens soley because of their ethnicity is neither compatible with the Constitution nor an effective way to make our nation more secure."[4]

The Okuras have spent their lives trying to overcome prejudice and discrimination. They would be the first to agree that constant vigilance is required if discrimination is to be held in check.

BIBLIOGRAPHY

Chapter 1

1. Durant, Will: The Story Of Civilization, I Our Oriental Heritage, Simon and Schuster, New York. 1954.
2. Kennedy, Paul: The Rise and Fall of the Great Powers. Vintage Books, New York. 1989.
3. Hosokawa, Bill: Nisei. The Quiet Americans, William Morrow and Company, Inc., New York. 1969.
4. Ichioka, Yuji: The Issei. The World of the First Generation Japanese Immigrants 1885-1924, The Free Press, New York. 1988.
5. Uyeda, Clifford: Suspended: Growing Up Asian in America, National Japanese American Historical Society, Inc., San Francisco, California. 2000.
6. Hosokawa, Bill: JACL In Quest Of Justice, William Morrow & Co., New York. 1982.

Chapter 2

1. Hosokawa, Bill: JACL In Quest of Justice.
2. Ibid.
3. Ibid.
4. Ibid.
5. Hosokawa, Bill: The Quiet Americans, William Morrow & Co., New York. 1942.
6. Uyeda, Clifford.
7. Chinese Exclusion Act. An act to execute certain treaty stipulations relating to Chinese. Forty-Seventh Congress of the United States. Chapter 126. May 6, 1882.
8. Hosokawa, Bill: JACL In Quest of Justice.
9. Hosokawa, Bill: The Quiet Americans.

10. Executive Order 9066. Signed by President Franklin Roosevelt, February 22, 1942. National Archives. Washington, D.C.

Chapter 3

1. Executive Order 9066.
2. Hosokawa, Bill: Nisei: The Quiet Americans.
3. Hosokawa, Bill: JACL in Quest Of Justice.
4. Hosakawa, Bill: Nisei. The Quiet Americans.
5. Ibid.
6. Ibid.
7. Burton, Farrell,Land, & Lord: Confinement and Ethnicity. An Overview of World War II Japanese American Relocation Sites, Western Archeological and Conservation Center, National Parks Service, Dept. of Interior, US Government Printing Office, Washington, 1999.
8. Ibid.
9. Hosokawa, Bill: Nisei: The Quiet Americans.
10. Ibid.
11. Hosokawa, Bill: JACL In Quest Of Justice.
12. Ibid.

Chapter 4

1. Burton, Farrell, Land, & Lord: Confinement and Ethnicity.
2. Uchida, Yoshiko: The InvisibleThread, Simon and Schuster, New York. 1991.
3. Hannon, James J: Nasakenai: (We Are Forsaken), Grossmont Press, San Diego, California. 1977.

Chapter 5
1. Wu, Frank H: Yellow. Race in America Beyond Black and White, Basic Books, New York. 2002.

Chapter 8

1. Wu, Frank H: Yellow. Race in America Beyond Black and White.

Chapter 9

1. Hosakawa, Bill: JACL in Quest of Justice.
2. Brown, Bertram: Personal Communication, January 2003.
3. Andrews, Susan: Personal Communication, January 1999.

Chapter 10

1. Joseph, James: Remaking America, Jossey-Bass, San Francisco, California. 1999.
2. The Washington Post. Washington, D.C. November 10, 2000.
3. Ibid.
4. The Washington Post. Washington, D.C. February 10, 2003.

ABOUT THE AUTHOR

After a fifty-year career in academic medicine, specializing in developmental pediatrics, Robert Kugel turned to writing biographies and some fiction. His career in academic medicine began with pediatrics, followed by fellowship training in child development and children with various developmental disabilities. His career was always combined with teaching and research in various medical schools. Throughout his career, which included service as a professor and later medical school dean in several university settings, he was always trying to understand how people cope with adversity of any kind. As an observer of the human condition and as a physician to children and their families, he brings a special insight to his writing.

Kugel now is retired though he continues to do some consulting. He is living in northern Virginia with his wife, Dorothy. He enjoys opera, photography, and collecting antique pewter. He has three daughters who have active careers in government, business and university teaching. In addition, he has two grandchildren.

www.ingramcontent.com/pod-product-compliance
Lightning Source LLC
Chambersburg PA
CBHW072207270326
41930CB00011B/2560